'OLD F

BY DENNIS WHEATLEY

NOVELS

The Launching of Roger Brook
The Shadow of Tyburn Tree
The Rising Storm
The Man Who Killed the King
The Dark Secret of Josephine
The Rape of Venice
The Sultan's Daughter
The Wanton Princess
Evil in a Mask
The Ravishing of Lady Mary Ware
The Irish Witch

The Scarlet Impostor
Faked Passports
The Black Baroness
V for Vengeance
Come Into My Parlour
Traitors' Gate
They Used Dark Forces

The Prisoner in the Mask
The Second Seal
Vendetta in Spain
Three Inquisitive People
The Forbidden Territory
The Devil Rides Out
The Golden Spaniard
Strange Conflict
Codeword—Golden Fleece
Dangerous Inheritance
Gateway to Hell

The Quest of Julian Day
The Sword of Fate
Bill for the Use of a Body

Black August
Contraband
The Island Where Time Stands Still
The White Witch of the South Seas

To the Devil—a Daughter
The Satanist

The Eunuch of Stamboul
The Secret War
The Fabulous Valley
Sixty Days to Live
Such Power is Dangerous
Uncharted Seas
The Man Who Missed the War
The Haunting of Toby Jugg
Star of Ill-Omen
They Found Atlantis
The Ka of Gifford Hillary
Curtain of Fear
Mayhem in Greece
Unholy Crusade
The Strange Story of Linda Lee
The Irish Witch
Desperate Measures

SHORT STORIES

Mediterranean Nights
Gunmen, Gallants and Ghosts

HISTORICAL

A Private Life of Charles II (*Illustrated by Frank C. Papé*)
Red Eagle (*The Story of the Russian Revolution*)

AUTOBIOGRAPHICAL

Stranger than Fiction (*War Papers for the Joint Planning Staff*)
Saturdays with Bricks

SATANISM

The Devil and all his works (*Illustrated in colour*)

Dennis Wheatley

'OLD ROWLEY'

A Very Private Life of Charles II

'Who is there?'
''Tis Old Rowley himself, ma'am.'

ARROW BOOKS

Arrow Books Limited
3 Fitzroy Square, London W1

An imprint of the Hutchinson Publishing Group

London Melbourne Sydney Auckland
Wellington Johannesburg and agencies
throughout the world

First published 1933
First Arrow edition 1962
This edition 1977

Made and printed in Great Britain
by The Anchor Press Ltd
Tiptree, Essex

ISBN 0 09 913980 4

Dedication

'It maketh me only the more ready to serve thee, with all the vigour that time hath left me, and all the loyalty that no time can take away.'

James Butler, Duke of Ormonde and Viceroy of Ireland. In a letter to Charles II acknowledging a warning of a plot to force his resignation, after an intimate knowledge of his master, as Child, Prince, Exile and King, for Fifty Years.

'Give me ten thousand good and loyal soldiers and subjects and I will soon drive all these rogues forth out of my Kingdom.'

Charles II, after his defeat at Worcester.

Thus, with these excellent sentiments before me, I offer this book to those loyal friends who stood by me in 1932.

DENNIS WHEATLEY

Contents

ONE

The Reason why the King 'went on his Travels'

THE Victorian Age being eminently Puritanical, it is not surprising that both Charles I and Charles II should have suffered at the hands of its historians. Most of us left our schools with the former docketed in our minds as a weak and stupid man, led into the oppression of his people by evil counsellors, a tyrant unfitted to govern, and one possessing most of the attributes of a really bad King. An impression which is only coloured by a sentimental regard engendered by the portraits of Van Dyck —where we see him as a handsome, melancholy man— and a knowledge of his tragic end.

Fortunately for those of us whose interest has survived the arctic-douche of school-taught history, original sources are available, and we are able to readjust our views.

The elder Charles may have been weak, but he certainly was not a tyrant, and with regard to his personality there are two points which our school books omit to mention—

and upon which the portraits of the Dutch Master are necessarily silent. In his youth he was cursed with a nervous stutter, a disability which he never quite got over, and later, although of pious habit, he was considered to be the most foul-mouthed man in his kingdom.

We may imagine him, then, at the age of twenty-nine, a little after one o'clock on the afternoon of May 29th, 1630, exclaiming to his friend and counsellor Thomas Wentworth:

'B-B-By my —— b-beard, Tom! —— my eyes, if 'tis not another b-b-boy!'

While in the adjoining room, or more probably the same apartment, for in those days all Royal Accouchements were actually witnessed by the principal persons of the State, Henrietta Maria had ceased her screaming and given birth to the dark-faced infant later to be known as Charles II—or, as his lewd and loving subjects preferred to call him, 'Old Rowley', the sobriquet being culled from the famous stallion of that name, owing to the obvious similarity of their masculine vigour.

Of the infancy of Charles II, little is recorded that is of interest, except that he had a strange and unaccountable fondness for a wooden billet, without which in his arms he would never go abroad, nor lie down in his bed. A characteristic which he maintained throughout his later life, excepting only that the consistency of the billet became changed for something of a softer nature.

In his early youth he was much at Hampton Court and Windsor, where the tedium of exercises in theology with old Brian Duppa, Bishop of Chichester, and in arithmetic with the famous mathematician Hobbs, was often lightened by excursions on the river. Something of his love of idle dreaming in after years may perhaps be attributed to those long summer afternoons of drowsy heat, when the Royal children in their gilded barge listened to the lapping of the waters in the quiet reaches of the Upper Thames.

From his father, who was the greatest art connoisseur in the Europe of his day, he must have derived much of his love of elegance and beauty—and it is not difficult to trace other outstanding qualities of his character to his grandparents.

From King James I he derived that enquiring mind which led to his lifelong interest in science and letters. From Jamie's wife, the gay and beautiful Anne of Denmark, his love of masques, company, and entertainments of every kind. From his maternal grandmother, the Italian Marie de Medici, the subtle brain and devious policy with which he held his own among the pitfalls of the Restoration—and from her husband, the brave and gallant Henry of Navarre, his personal courage, his astute statesmanship, and his amorous propensities.

It is said that Charles was a quick, intelligent child, and there is no knowing what pearls of wisdom may not have fallen on his youthful ears from men such as Sir Thomas Browne, Izaak Walton, Herrick and Edmund Waller, all of whom were visitors to his father's court. Inigo Jones and his son-in-law John Webb would also have been well known to the boy, and those famous architects doubtless did much to pave the way that was to lead him later to be so munificent a patron to their successor Wren and the decorator Grinling Gibbons.

One fears, however, that more of the time which he spent in the company of his parents was employed in listening to discourses on the religious problems of the day. Such, for example, as the burning question which agitated the whole of the three Kingdoms, as to whether the table with the sacraments should be placed at the east end of the church or in the middle—and doubtless he was glad enough to escape into the garden for a good game of pirates or Red Indians with his small companions.

Among the latter was George Villiers, second Duke of Buckingham, whose father had fallen by the hand of the assassin Felton seven months after his son was born. George was some two years older than Charles and of a merry, frolicsome disposition. With his wild and reckless nature, we may be sure that he led the younger boy into many a scrape, but it is probable that Charles needed little leading.

At the age of eight we find Charles receiving a letter from the Queen—a woman whose dark good looks were somewhat marred by her protruding teeth—upon the horrid subject of medicine. 'Charles, I am sore,' she writes, 'that I must begin my first letter with chiding you because I heere that you will not take your phisick,' and Charles, already, it seems, showing some signs of budding wit, writes to his tutor, the Earl of Newcastle, upon the same subject, 'I would not have you take too much phisick, for it doth allwaies make me worse, and I think it will do the like with you.'

No finer governor than Newcastle could have been chosen for the boy. He was the finest horseman of his day, a great lover of music and had abundance of sound common sense. Two excellent precepts of his to Charles survive: 'Put money in thy purse and keep it', and 'Study men—not books'. The former it was not in Charles' nature to carry out, but from the latter no man derived more profit.

It was the Queen's delight to train him 'to a wonderful civility', and in his later life he never failed in a most perfect courtesy in his dealings with every class of people. By this time, however, Henrietta Maria had more serious things to think of, for the troubles of the Royal Family were about to begin in earnest.

The mismanagement by the magnificent Buckingham in the early years of the reign had caused the lowering of our prestige abroad and the growth of discontent at home;

but by his death, Charles had become free to choose his own ministers.

Archbishop Laud and Thomas Wentworth, Earl of Strafford, were the two men to whom he entrusted the destinies of the State. Both were able men, and both acted entirely in concurrence with the King's own views. Their duty, as all three saw it, was to stem the tide of Sectarian Nonconformity which had become a definite menace to the established religion of the land.

In this they came immediately into conflict with Parliament, and it is well at this juncture to consider just what the House of Commons was at that date.

Not more than one out of every hundred of the population had an actual voice in the election of the Members, and therefore they could no more be said actually to represent the country than the nobles at court or a mass meeting of unemployed watermen. They were simply a body of men drawn from a certain strata of society.

A considerable number of them were small country gentry whose families had been in the forefront of the revolt against Rome, and who were therefore filled with a Calvinistic fire. An equally large number, since the factor of commerce had now begun to enter seriously into the problems of the country, were engaged in trade or banking. The banking interests, it is well known, have always been largely in Quaker hands, and so it was a natural corollary that the Zealots and Industrials should become fused into a solid block to resist the policy of the Crown.

Such men as John Hampden unquestionably did much to establish the liberties of the English people by their staunch resistance of abuses, but it should be remembered that those abuses were no personal tyrannies introduced by Charles—they were forms of government inherited from a line of sovereigns, including Henry VIII and Elizabeth, whom we have been taught to regard as great.

Yet if the more honest of the Commons had the good of the people at heart, so also had the King. Time after time we find him legislating to protect the common people from the profiteers—butchers, bakers, brewers, drapers, gardeners, jewellers, and inn-holders, to name but a few, all came up against his ordinances to prevent fraud and ensure fair standards of weight and quality to the consumer. It was indeed very largely his anxiety to ensure a decent standard of living to the masses which gained him the bitter enmity of the capitalist classes and lost him his throne.

His kindly thought for his poorer subjects is well expressed in the proclamation by which he repealed the Lord's Day Observance Act. 'If these times be taken from them, the meaner sort who labour all the weeke should have no recreation at all to refresh their spirits, and therefore we do order that after attending prayers, every man shall be allowed to amuse himself in any decent way which he may choose.' His people got their Sunday games, but the measure earned him the undying hatred of the Puritans.

The war therefore was waged by the middle-class capitalists, who wished for greater opportunities to put money in their pockets and to force their stricter form of worship on the country—against the Court, who desired to maintain its ancient privileges and enforce the doctrine of the Established Church.

A little before Charles II was eight years old, the Scottish Bishops drew up a new prayer book under the auspices of Laud. The Scots rejected the book and many thousands of them signed a National Covenant, swearing to resist the enforcement of it with their lives. By March, 1639, they had taken up arms and under the leadership of Leslie surprised Edinburgh Castle. This was the opening scene of the Grand Rebellion.

A few months later a settlement was reached, but by the following year they were in revolt again, and this time crossed the Tweed in force. Charles took the field against them, but after a certain amount of marching and counter-marching the quarrel was patched up, and he dashed south to attend to his affairs in London.

In November, 1640, he summoned the 'Long' Parliament, which proved to be his doom, and its first action was the impeachment of his Minister, Strafford. The Earl defended himself nobly and well, the impeachment broke down and a bill of attainder was introduced. To become a death warrant it needed the King's signature, and at first he refused to sign. The results were tumultuous assemblies in London, constant deputations from the Parliament, and a thousand insults flung against the Queen, who, as a foreigner and a Frenchwoman, was considered to be Charles' evil genius. Young Charles, who was then ten years old, must have heard the howling of the mob beneath the palace windows. Open threats were made against the persons of the Royal Family, and after days of terrible indecision the King yielded, sending his loyal servant to the scaffold.

That he was under grievous pressure at the time we see from his own words, 'If my own person were in danger, I would gladly venture it to save Lord Strafford's life—but seeing that my wife, children, and all my kingdom are concerned in it—I am forced to give way to it,' and no one has ever accused this King of cowardice at least.

The tragedy of the sacrifice was its futility. Parliament had tasted blood and it only served to whet their appetite for more. Laud and Finch were immediately impeached, and measure after measure hurried through the Commons during the following year, until, in the early summer of 1642, the King felt that, unless his authority was to be lost completely, he must make a definite stand.

Accordingly he visited the House in person for the

purpose of arresting the five most fractious members, but the attempt was a failure, for they had been warned in time and gone into hiding. Parliament took refuge in the precincts of the City and on June 10th the King left London, never to return until seven years later he entered it a prisoner.

His eldest son, a rather fat-faced boy of twelve, with dark hair curling at the ends, rode in his train; also his second son, James, Duke of York, who was then nine years of age. Henrietta Maria, as a daughter of France, retired to the Court of her nativity.

The King, having been refused admission to Hull, which closed its gates against him in sympathy with Parliament, went to York. There he began to collect his forces; then moving south, and having had the words emblazoned upon it—'Render unto Cæsar the things that are Cæsar's', he raised the Royal Standard at Nottingham on August 23rd, 1642.

A rough disposition of the parties can be gathered by dividing the Kingdom with a line from Southampton to Hull. Parliament drew its principal support from the towns and counties to the east of this, while those to the west stood mainly for the King.

Two months later the first collision between the opposing forces took place at Edge Hill, and the two boys witnessed the battle from a neighbouring eminence. They had been placed in the care of no less interesting a person than the famous Dr. Harvey, who discovered the circulation of the blood, and owing to his studious nature received their baptism of fire. A large cannon ball bounding by at fifty miles an hour recalled him from his book to his responsibilities, and he quickly removed his charges to a safer distance.

The battle was indecisive, but during the night the Parliamentarians withdrew and the way was left open for the King to advance on Oxford, which he proceeded to occupy, and which became his main headquarters for a number of years.

During the first year of hostilities, fortune favoured the Royalist Cause, but Cromwell, who was then by no means so important as he was later to become, had been busy in the Eastern Counties raising and training his Ironsides, who afterwards played so large a part in the Parliamentary victories.

Young Buckingham, as may be imagined, was wholeheartedly for the King. He showed conspicuous gallantry in storming the Parliamentary stronghold of Lichfield, for which piece of bravery Parliament promptly confiscated his estates, but that they were not unreasonably bitter at this time is shown by their generosity in returning his lands to him on the plea that he was only sixteen years of age. He was with the Court at Oxford for some time, where his mad pranks infuriated the elderly Dons, but in 1646 he went on the 'Grand Tour', and most of his time during the next two years was spent in Rome and Florence.

The Civil War had quickly spread to the other Kingdoms, but towards the end of 1643 the tide had begun to turn in favour of Parliament. The loyal Ormonde was forced to conclude an armistice in Ireland, and although the gallant Montrose counselled fighting on, the King entered into negotiations with the rebel Scots through Hamilton.

The fanaticism of the Covenanters was at the root of the trouble throughout the whole of the Civil War. They had been the first to take up arms against the King, and it was they who sold him to his enemies in the end. In this instance they were still negotiating with Charles when they entered into an alliance with the English Parliament, the latter agreeing to accept the Covenant.

Parliament brought Laud to trial, but found themselves in considerable difficulty since all his actions had had the approval and sanction of the King. In desperation they urged that even if no one of his acts could be proved to be treasonable, in bulk they must be so. Upon which counsel for the defence exclaimed with spirit, 'I cry you mercy—'tis the first time that an hundred black rabbits did make one black horse,' but his logic was unavailing, a bill of attainder was passed, this time without the sanction of the King, and Laud followed Strafford to the block on Tower Hill.

It was during these dark days early in 1644 that young Charles and James, sick unto death of living in the cramped quarters of an Oxford college, asked their father when they might go home again—and he replied so sadly, 'Alas, my poor children, I have no home to go to.'

In March that year, the King sent Charles for safety into the West Country, and although he was then only fourteen, he was made the head of an organization to treat with Parliament, but his overtures were unsuccessful.

In the summer, Leslie with his Scots joined Fairfax in the Northern Counties and the Royalists began to lose ground in that area, then in July, having united forces with Cromwell and Manchester, the Roundheads inflicted a crushing defeat upon the Cavaliers under Newcastle and the too dashing Prince Rupert, at Marston Moor near York. A further defeat of the Royalists followed at Newbury in October.

In 1645, the Parliamentary Army was completely re-organized and Oliver Cromwell definitely came to the front as its principal commander. In the June of that year, his new levies, strongly seasoned with his now veteran Ironsides, inflicted a final and decisive defeat upon all that was left of the King's organized forces at Naseby. The rest of the year and the spring of the next were spent in quelling such last scattered forces of the Crown as still offered a desperate resistance up and down the country. So ends the first Civil War.

Charles, a little before his sixteenth birthday, was compelled to seek safety in the Scilly Isles, and in March started upon those travels which were not to have a successful ending until more than fourteen years later.

Parliament sent him a polite note, suggesting that if he cared to return to England they would 'appoint a place where he could live securely', but the dark, good-looking young stripling and his advisers were doubtless adequately informed regarding the legend of the spider and the fly. A polite but ambiguous reply was therefore despatched to His Majesty's Most Untrustworthy Commons. After six weeks in the Scillies he removed to Jersey and thence to join his mother at the Court of France.

The residence of the Queen and her daughter, the little Henrietta, at the latter, does little honour to the French. The *great* Cardinal, de Richelieu, was dead; and in his room the miserly Italian—Mazarin—had become the all-powerful Minister to the Queen Regent, Anne of Austria, if not actually her husband by a secret marriage. Owing to his parsimony the English Queen suffered virtual destitution. She was housed in rooms almost lacking in furniture, and, during the winter, was often without a fire or even sufficient blankets for the beds.

It may be said in palliation, however, that this niggardliness was not solely directed against the English refugees, since Mazarin, who controlled everything, allowed the young King Louis XIV and his brother Phillip only one pair of stockings apiece at a time, and the boys complained that they 'could not lie comfortable in bed because the sheets were so patched and darned'. Moreover, the fact that Henrietta Maria was the daughter of Henri IV of France did not make her any the less difficult and troublesome a guest.

For Charles, it is probable that there were compensations in this, his first visit to the French capital. Perhaps the blood of his amorous grandfather the 'vert galant' was stirring in his veins, or perhaps it was just Paris—in May. In any case it seems more than likely that somewhere about this time he first sampled those joys which were ever afterwards to be his ruling passion.

It may be that the younger Charles was toying in pleasant dalliance with some flushed young French girl at the very moment when the elder surrendered his person into the keeping of the Scots at Newcastle, since this event took place in the May of that same year.

In September a vote was taken 'that the King should be disposed of as both Houses of Parliament shall see fit', and on January 30th, 1647, he was sold by his countrymen to the English Commissioners. He was taken to Holmby House in Northamptonshire, and there seized in the following June, upon the instigation of Cromwell who feared to leave his person in the hands of the

Moderates, by one Cornet Joyce, formerly a tailor. From Holmby House the King was conveyed to Hampton Court, thence he escaped to the Isle of Wight and took refuge in Carisbrooke Castle, but he might have spared himself the pains of his flight. Robin Hammond, the governor of Carisbrooke, was 'Dear Robin' to Cromwell and could be trusted to see that the King did not escape further afield.

In January, 1648, a suggestion was made to impeach the King and the second Civil War burst into flame. Laud's execution had shocked and horrified all those who still clung to the Established Church. He was after all a prelate, and they knew him moreover to be an honest man. In addition the Army was now definitely becoming the ruling power and England has ever been averse to a military dictatorship.

Sympathy was expressed on all sides for the King. A large portion of the Fleet rebelled against the Parliament, the Scottish Cavaliers invaded England from the North, and both Kent and Essex took up arms to save His Majesty.

It was probably in order to be in closer touch with the Royalist portion of the Navy that the younger Charles left Paris for the Hague, but his removal from the French capital was expedited by Mazarin and the fact that his mother ruled him with a rod of iron. She even seized upon the allowance which the French Government had reluctantly made him, and doled him out a few pennies pocket money at a time, so that it was said of him, 'He hath not ten pistoles which he can call his own.'

Cromwell was too firmly seated in the saddle by this time for the Royalist cause to have much chance of permanent success. The mutiny in the Fleet was quelled, the loyal Scots defeated at Preston in August, Colchester captured after a truly heroic resistance, and the risings in the South speedily crushed.

In a forlorn hope the Earl of Holland raised the Standard of the King in Surrey, but the Cavaliers were routed and dispersed, Buckingham and his brother Francis Villiers were among them, the latter meeting his death in a skirmish near Nonsuch. The Duke escaped, but nearly lost his life by an accident, the low branch of a tree catching his helmet and completely reversing it upon his head, so that he would have died of strangulation but for the prompt aid of his servant.

Later he took refuge in a house which was soon after surrounded by the enemy. With desperate courage he ordered the gates to be flung open, galloped at full tilt out of the courtyard, killed the commander of the Parliamentary troops, hacked his way through the rest, and escaped unharmed to the coast; afterwards joining Charles who was hovering with a few loyal ships in the Channel.

At the end of the year the King was taken to Windsor,

and in January '49 a high court was set up to judge him. He appeared before his accusers on the 20th of the month, and demanded to know by what authority they had brought him to trial.

'In the name of Parliament assembled and all the good people of England,' was the reply of Bradshaw, the president of the tribunal.

Lady Fairfax, the wife of the Parliamentary General, who was present as a spectator, sprang to her feet and cried, 'It is a lie! Not a half—nay, not a quarter of the people of England.'

That she spoke truly was evidenced by the fact that before they could bring the King to trial, even his old enemy the Parliament, from which all men of moderate views had long since withdrawn, had to be purged by Colonel Pride of no less than two-thirds of its remaining members. So that it was now a mockery of its former self and only consisted of some half hundred embittered Puritans.

The Royalist reaction had come too late and the sympathies of the great mass of the nation were of little avail. As in the case of all Revolutions, power had passed into the hands of a small group of Extremists and the King was doomed.

He answered his accusers with quiet majesty, 'It is not my case alone, it is the freedom and liberties of the people of England—and do you pretend what you will,

I stand more for their liberties. For if power without law may make laws—I do not know what subject he is in England, who may be sure of his life, or anything that he calls his own.'

After that bold declaration his dignity forbade that he should plead or endeavour to defend himself before what he considered to be the arbitrary tribunal of his enemies.

Charles at the Hague did the only thing that lay in his power. He sent a blank sheet of paper with his signature and seal attached, that they might make what terms they would upon it, if only they would spare his father's life—but nothing could turn the fanatics from their purpose.

Where our War Office stands now, then stood the old Palace of Whitehall, and from a first floor window of it, upon the winter morning of January 30th, 1649, the King stepped out into the drifting snowflakes that swirled about the black-draped scaffold. As he went so bravely to his tragic end, every blind was drawn; and strange as it may seem, although he had been condemned as tyrant—traitor—murderer, the streets were thronged—not with a howling mob thirsting for his blood—but with a silent and a weeping people.

TWO

The Scottish Adventure and 'Worcester Fight'

DURING the spring of '49 Charles remained at the Hague, and in those months preceding his nineteenth birthday, two events of major importance took place. He lost his father and begot a son.

The child, afterwards the ill-fated James, Duke of Monmouth, was born on April 9th at Rotterdam, the mother being Lucy Walter, or Mrs. Barlow, as it seems she preferred to be called.

She was a lovely brown-haired Welsh girl, with beautiful eyes and fair white skin, plump and amorous—but a fool. She was Charles' first great passion and he loved her very dearly, so much so that there are strong grounds for supposing that he actually married her. Fuller, Bishop of Lincoln, often affirmed that he had performed the ceremony, and an innkeeper at Liège swore that the marriage took place and was consummated at his house, he and his wife being 'eye and ear witnesses of it'. Yet Charles himself sturdily denied this in after years.

There is little doubt but that Lucy was a slut. Charles had first met her during his stay in Wales, and she followed him to the Hague with the deliberate intention of becoming his mistress. She had already been living with Colonel Robert Sidney, and in fact Monmouth bore such a striking resemblance to the Colonel that many people believed the latter to be the father of the child. The resemblance proves nothing, and Charles himself appears to have been perfectly satisfied that Monmouth was his son, but Lucy's infidelities became so flagrantly open when the King was in Scotland, that he was compelled to abandon her on his return.

Her reign may have been brief but at least we may assume that while it lasted she did much to take the young King's thoughts off his troubles, and that in later years he was able to recall with pleasure those happy days, wrested from the conflicting councils of his advisers, when with her for company he picnicked in the shady glades of Den Bosch, or on the nearby beach at Scheveningen.

His principal counsellor at this time, and one who was to continue so for many years to come, was Edward Hyde, a stalwart Wiltshireman and able lawyer, who afterwards became Earl of Clarendon, and in his declining years indited the many volumes that constitute his *History of the Great Rebellion*.

Buckingham was also with the King. His estates had been confiscated again, but Parliament had allowed his faithful steward Traylman to remain at York House, the Duke's great London mansion; and since Traylman employed himself in smuggling out of the country a large portion of the magnificent collection of pictures which had been gathered together by the first Duke, George, unlike so many of the others for whom the King had to provide, managed to support himself upon the proceeds of these treasures during his exile.

The Dutch Government, fearing to embroil themselves with Cromwell, intimated to Charles that they were considerably embarrassed by his presence, he therefore left the Hague in June, proceeding in the leisurely fashion of the time, by way of Rotterdam, Breda, Antwerp, and Brussels, to Paris. In the French capital he found himself an equally unwelcome guest, and Jersey being the only portion of his dominions which still held for the Crown, he took ship thither, arriving in September.

Something of the financial difficulties which were a source of constant anxiety to him during the whole of his exile, may be judged from the fact that he arrived in the Island with a court of some three hundred people, and only three hundred pistoles wherewith to pay the passage of them all.

Ormonde meanwhile had once more raised the Standard of the King in Ireland, and Cromwell arrived to crush the revolt in July. By the time Charles reached Jersey, his Irish Royalist had been defeated and the Lord Protector had begun his savage progress of extermination.

The Civil War in England had been remarkably free from the partisan acts of barbarity which make such terrible reading in those annals concerning the internecine strife of other nations. In Ireland, however, it was a very different matter. From the time of the massacre at Drogheda in September until the following spring, Cromwell marched through the land, hanging, burning, and slaughtering with an incredible ferocity. If any extenuation can be pleaded it must be upon the grounds that in this instance he was fighting against the detested 'Papists', who to a man of his deep religious convictions were definitely not human, but the very emissaries of hell.

The King's second stay in Jersey, like his first, was brief. News was received that Parliament was fitting out a powerful fleet to bring the island into subjection, so Charles was forced to take ship once more. After a great storm in which he narrowly escaped being wrecked, he landed in France, and hurrying through that inhospitable country, sought refuge in Breda, where he had previously been so well received.

The Scots had proclaimed him King at Edinburgh within a week of his father's death, but Argyll and the

Covenanters still controlled the country. A premature attempt by the Scottish Cavaliers to regain Scotland for the King was defeated in the following year, and their great leader, the gallant Montrose, having sought shelter with the Macleod of Assynt, was sold by him and paraded through the streets of Edinburgh on May 21st, 1650, on his way to execution.

The Covenanters, however, were greatly disappointed in the English Parliament. The victorious Commons were beginning to dispute among themselves, and the old Industrialist party, now called 'Independents', whose ranks contained most of the Army Commanders who had fought in the late war, were definitely gaining the upper hand. It occurred to the Covenanters that if they could gain possession of the person of Charles, they might yet be able to assist their allies the Zealots to overthrow the 'Independents', and force their stricter morality on the land.

A deputation of Scottish Commissioners therefore arrived at the Hague with an invitation for the King to place himself in their hands, and were received with becoming gravity. The bottles of Rhenish and Schnapps were pushed in the cupboard, Lucy was told that she must get herself a dress with a higher neck, and the collection of scalliwags, opportunists, and serious loyalists who composed the Court, proceeded to listen to a number of sermons of unusual length.

The fact that the Covenanters had just killed his devoted servant Montrose, together with their previous conduct, naturally made Charles extremely sceptical of their new found loyalty, and the conditions which they proposed were harsh in the extreme. He knew too that they only wished to use him for their own ends, but, after having listened to much conflicting advice from his council, he decided to take a chance on being able to use them for his.

It may well be that the words of his grandfather, Henri IV of France, recurred to him at that time, for was it not the wily Bernais who in a very similar situation decided to pacify his rebellious subjects once and for all by declaring, 'Ah, well—Paris is worth a mass.'

In June 1650, therefore, Charles arrived in Scotland, ostensibly at all events a meek and sober member of the Kirk. Knowing as he must have done the completely alien nature of this dour folk to the natural gaiety of his twenty years, the fact that he ever went on this adventure shows his determination to leave no chance untried which might regain his Crown.

Had he ever been brought to trial for the undoubted immorality of his later years, no fair-minded jury could have failed to make a recommendation to mercy, in consideration of that incredible time which he spent in Scotland. Indeed, had he actually served a sentence of imprisonment his situation could hardly have been worse, for his life was ordered as strictly as that of any Benedictine monk. The long-faced elders would not even allow him to walk abroad on the Sabbath, spies were set about his person to report the least attempt at merriment or joke—cards and dancing were forbidden and fast-days observed with such rigour that the poor young man was compelled to listen to no less than six sermons in a single day. Yet such was his tact and patience, that apart from one outbreak, he bore it all with apparent equanimity, while preparing in secret his principal design.

While the Covenanters connived at Buckingham's dissolute course of life because he agreed to advise the King to rely wholly upon their guidance, and sent deputations to Charles, to reprove him, and request that he 'at least close the window', when he was found in converse with a wench, the King was steadily gaining adherents among the Moderates by his personal charm, and succeeded in getting them to crown him at Scone in January, 1651. He now felt himself strong enough to dispense with the treacherous Argyll, and proceeded to manœuvre the Scottish Army into some semblance of activity.

During the previous summer, the Covenanters had so feared Charles' popularity with the Army that they had refused to allow him to join it when Cromwell marched north against them. The Lord Protector had gained a sweeping victory at Dunbar in September, and the fact that the King had not been defeated in person was now all to the good.

Unfortunately for Charles, the Navy, which his father had been largely instrumental in bringing to such a high standard for the times, was now turned against him, and holding the seas under the gallant Blake, prevented friends and assistance reaching him from abroad. His policy of peaceful penetration, however, proved equal to the task of reconciling the various factions among the Scots, and at the head of considerable forces, he invaded England in the late summer of 1651.

This was the one attempt made by Charles to regain his throne by force of arms and it might well have succeeded had he had with him the loyal Highlanders of Montrose. Instead he was saddled with dour old Leslie, who when the King enquired why he looked so gloomy at an inspection of the troops, replied, 'Gallant as the Army might appear, he knew it well, and was certain that it would not fight.'

The King marched south to Worcester, and there gave battle to the Parliamentary troops. Charles showed great personal courage, leading the first charge of the Cavaliers with such impetuous gallantry, that even Cromwell's veteran Ironsides were temporarily broken. He had two horses shot under him and was one of the last to leave the field, refusing to retire until, after four hours of strenuous engagement, he found his troops were being scattered in all directions.

He then fell back upon the city of Worcester, and with calm courage endeavoured to rally his forces, but the Cromwellians entering the town in great numbers, it became obvious that any attempt to convert the rout into an orderly retreat must prove hopeless.

As usual, the counsels of his principal supporters were divided. The greater number were for his joining Leslie, who true to his own prophecy had only played the part of looker-on, and therefore had been able to withdraw his 3,000 cavalry in good order. But at all times of real crisis Charles was very capable of making up his own mind and he had had enough of the Covenanters to last him a lifetime. His principal embarrassment was the number of people he had with him, for, as he afterwards said, 'I began to think of the best way of saving myself, and though I could not get them to stand with me against the enemy, I could not get rid of them now I had a mind to it.' Eventually, however, having persuaded the majority of his companions to seek their own safety and leave him to seek his as best he might, he took the road to Kidderminster, with Buckingham, Derby, Lauderdale, Wilmot, and others of his immediate following, numbering some sixty persons in all.

At nightfall they reached Kinver Heath where they got hopelessly lost; then in the dawn, when they were so utterly exhausted with their many hours in the saddle that rest became imperative, a Mr. Charles Giffard took charge of the party and led them to the ruined monastery of Whiteladies.

Here they learned that Leslie and his three thousand were close by at Tong Castle, and further attempts were made to persuade Charles to join him, but the King had very wisely decided never to place himself in the power of the Covenanters again. Buckingham and the rest, with the exception of Lord Wilmot, joined Leslie. How right Charles was in refusing to be of their company, we see from his own words when he afterwards related his adventure, 'As I did before believe, they did not reach six miles after they had got to them, but they were all routed by a single troop of horse, which shows that my opinion was not wrong, in not sticking to men who had run away.'

Leslie's troops having scattered, Buckingham, after passing through a series of hairbreadth escapes hardly less remarkable than those which befell the King, reached London, and his sojourn in the capital shows the audacious character of this versatile rogue. Instead of going into hiding he bought himself a Jack Pudding's coat and a hat adorned with cock's feathers and a fox's tail, then his face bedaubed with lamp-black, he disported himself on a stage erected near Charing Cross, attended by violins and a number of puppet players.

In this strange guise he carried on a lively trade in ballads of his own composition and quack medicines, gaining meanwhile a shrewd insight into the trend of events and the temper of the people.

Despite the fact that his disguise included a patch over one eye, he was a fine figure of a man, and who of all people in the world should be filled with carnal desire at the sight of his sturdy limbs but Bridget, General Ireton's wife, and daughter to no less a person than the Lord Protector.

The lady, little guessing the identity of the stalwart mountebank, sent for him to come to her by night, and one can well imagine the mixed feelings of the young Duke upon receiving this dangerous rendezvous. Should he go—chance discovery, and perhaps his life—or should he seek safety from the amorous lady in flight? His love of adventure got the better of his discretion, and he decided to keep the assignation, but in disguise.

Upon his arrival at the house, Bridget offered him so tempestuous a welcome that even he was scared. To go to bed with the young woman there and then meant certain recognition, so with ready wit he excused himself by making the awful revelation that he was a Jew, and saying that his religion strictly forbade him obliging any Christian woman. For the moment Cromwell's daughter was at a loss, but even this did not deter her from her purpose, and she requested him to come to her again upon the following night.

When he arrived, what was his horror to discover that Bridget had enlisted the services of a learned Rabbi, who proceeded immediately to assure him that he had been wrongly instructed in the Jewish faith. But poor Mrs. Ireton had gone to all her trouble in vain, for seeing no other way out of this desperate situation, Buckingham drew his cloak about him and fled into the night.

Charles, meanwhile, had been for many days in almost hourly risk of capture. At Whiteladies, the Penderels, a poor family of Catholic woodcutters who tenanted the house, appear upon the scene. There were five brothers, Richard, Humphrey, William (who lived at Boscobel close by) and two others, and it was largely owing to their loyalty that Charles eluded the Roundheads, who were thick as flies about the countryside during the first days of his flight.

It was at once decided that the King must be disguised. So they dressed him in a pair of grey cloth breeches, a leather doublet, green jerkin, and a greasy old steeple hat. Lord Wilmot hacked off his dark curls with a carving knife, while Richard Penderel trimmed them with a pair of shears, and Charles, laughing, blacked his own face with soot from the chimney. Then he was given a billhook to carry, and as they considered it too dangerous for him to remain in the house, turned out to hide as best he could in a nearby wood called Spring Coppice.

The weather was cold and wet, the King utterly exhausted from lack of sleep, and it must have been a miserable day that he spent on the damp ground, the rain dripping through the trees and only a single blanket for cover. He started up from an uneasy doze when Elizabeth Yates, a relative of the Penderels, was sent to him with food, and fearful at finding a woman in the secret of his identity exclaimed, 'Good woman! can you be faithful to a distressed Cavalier,' to which she loyally replied, 'Yes, sir, I had rather die than discover you.'

The early hours of the night were passed at the house of old Mrs. Penderel, Hobbal Grange; the old lady giving thanks to God that he had blessed her with five stalwart sons, that they might succour the King in his extremity, and here it was decided that the King should take the name of William Jackson. Charles was in favour of trying to reach London, but the others dissuaded him from it, and to quote his own words, 'A new decision was taken, which was to get over the Severn into Wales, and so get either to Swansea or some other seaport town that I knew had commerce with France.'

As a first step Richard and the King set out for a house called Madeley, the property of a Mr. Wolfe. Upon the way they were nearly shot by a miller who mistook them for thieves, and had to run for their lives. This adventure nearly proved the end of the wretched Charles. It was forty hours since he had slept, he was in a high fever from exposure, and had been compelled to throw away his shoes because his feet were so terribly galled. It seemed impossible for him to stagger further, yet with the help and encouragement of the faithful Richard he managed to reach his destination.

Richard was then sent ahead to sound Mr. Wolfe, who said at once that he would not incur the danger of harbouring a known Royalist 'unless it were the King himself'. Richard made a clean breast of the matter, upon which the old gentlemen replied, 'That he would be willing to venture all he had in the world to secure the King,' an answer that caused Charles considerable uneasiness, but he decided to chance Wolfe's loyalty and had no reason to regret it.

The house being considered unsafe, the King was concealed under the hay in a nearby barn. There he spent the remainder of the night and the following day, then being advised against the plan of crossing the Severn as too dangerous, he decided to return to Boscobel.

Fearing a fresh encounter with the shot-gun of the miller, they decided to recross the stream further along and now it was the sturdy Richard who broke down. Bursting into tears he declared that he could not swim, and urged the King to go on without him, but Charles, his courage renewed by rest and sleep, assured him that he would help him over somehow and boldly plunged into the stream.

Arrived at Boscobel once more, they breakfasted, and Charles learning that a Colonel Careless, who had led the last charge of the Cavaliers at Worcester, lay concealed close by, sent for him. It was decided that the two should spend the day together in the woods, and in the leafy branches of the Royal Oak Charles lay concealed while the Roundhead troopers searched the undergrowth below. The Cromwellians knew that he was somewhere in the immediate vicinity, so the King and Careless spent some anxious hours, hardly daring to shift their position when they were seized with cramp, or sore and aching from the knobbly nature of their perch.

When darkness fell, Careless killed a sheep and the King was helping to dismember it, when to his horror the owner appeared, catching them redhanded. But upon the man learning that the meat was for a fugitive Cavalier, and perhaps having more than a suspicion as to the Cavalier's identity, he smiled and refused all payment for the animal.

That night and the following day, Charles lay concealed at Boscobel. The next, Humphrey Penderel returned from paying his taxes at Shipnal and announced that a reward of £1,000 had been offered for the capture of the King, and it was in this notice that he was described so vividly as 'A tall black man, above two yards high.'

Learning that Wilmot was in hiding at Mosley, in the house of a Mr. Whitgreave, he decided on joining him there. His feet were still so badly galled that he was unable to walk, so the Penderels procured an old mill horse upon which he made the journey, all five brothers acting as an escort.

Father Huddlestone, a Roman Catholic priest, received Charles in a field near Mosley and led them to the house, where Whitgreave not knowing which of the weary mud-stained party to salute, Wilmot made the King known with the words, 'This is my master, your master, and the master of us all.'

The King's blistered feet were bathed while he sat before a welcome fire, munching a biscuit and sipping a glass of wine. The difficulties of his situation were discussed and nothing daunted he declared, 'That if it would please God to send him an army of 10,000 good and loyal soldiers and subjects, he feared not to expel all these rogues forth out of his kingdom.'

Two days were spent under Mr. Whitgreave's friendly roof, but on the second morning Father Huddlestone was forced to hide him in his own priest's hole, since the Roundheads paid a surprise visit to the house.

The project of heading for London was revived, and Wilmot went to Bentley, the house of Colonel Lane, to ask his advice and assistance. Lane considered it too dangerous, but helpfully suggested that since his sister was about to set out on a visit to her cousin at Bristol, the King might accompany her in the guise of a servant.

Accordingly the following night, with a bag of sweets in his pocket which Mr. Whitgreave's mother had pressed upon him because 'he was but a boy', he removed to Bentley, and in the morning set out with Miss Lane riding pillion behind him.

They had not been two hours upon the road when the horse cast a shoe, and at the village smithy, while the damage was being repaired, Charles asked for news. The smith replied that 'he had not yet heard if that rogue Charles Stuart were taken', upon which the King with subtle wit remarked 'If he were, he deserved to be hanged more than all the rest for bringing in the Scots.'

A little further on their road they encountered a large body of Roundheads who had halted by the wayside to rest their horses, but the King, trusting only in his servant's clothes for disguise, rode boldly through them with the pretty Miss Lane perched on the back of his saddle.

They broke the journey that night at Long Marston, and Charles had to fend for himself in the servants' quarters. As he was seated by the kitchen fire, the cook asked him to wind up the jack, and he made such a mess of the business that the woman cried angrily, 'What countryman are you, that you know not how to wind a jack?' but he soothed her with the apt reply, 'I am but a poor tenant's son of Colonel Lane's in Gloucestershire, and 'tis seldom that we see roast meat.'

The following night they put up at the Crown Inn at Cirencester, and again Charles had to make the best of a hard bed and servants' fare, but the next evening they successfully completed their hazardous journey and reached Mrs. Norton's house at Abbots Leigh.

Here, once more, he was quartered with the servants, but Jane Lane told her relatives that the poor boy was suffering from an ague, sent him some soup from the dinner-table, and secured him a separate room. Yet her kindness was nearly his undoing, for a Dr. George who had been Charles' chaplain was present, and since he fancied himself as a doctor, insisted on visiting the invalid. Fortunately he failed to recognize the King, as was also the case with one of the servants who had been a trooper in his own guards at Worcester. ''Tis said that I resemble him,' declared Charles boldly upon discovering this. 'Nay,' declared the man, 'he is three inches taller at least, and I'll wager thee on it.' Needless to say the bet was not accepted.

The following morning as he removed his hat on Miss Lane's passing through the hall, Pope the butler guessed his identity but proved a loyal and capable adherent. On his suggestion, Wilmot, who had been following at a distance, was sent to Colonel Francis Wyndham at Trent in the hope that he might be able to afford shelter for the King, and Pope himself went off to Bristol to try and secure a ship, and thus get him safely out of the country.

The week-end was spent at Abbots Leigh, and Pope returned, his efforts having met with no success, but Colonel Wyndham was willing to receive the King, and the trouble now was to get Charles out of the house. Mrs. Norton had miscarried of a still-born child and it was difficult for Jane Lane to leave her in such circumstances. This problem was solved by Pope, at whose suggestion Jane produced a forged letter, purporting to have come from her father with the news that he was dangerously ill. Having thus excused her hurried departure she set off again with Charles, spent the night at Castle Cary, where Lord Hertford's steward found them temporary accommodation, and the next evening delivered her fugitive King safely into the hands of Colonel Wyndham.

At Trent, a number of the servants were in the secret, so Charles was able to shelter there for several days in the first comfort he had known since before Worcester. Colonel Giles Strangeways, a relative of Colonel Wyndham's, was then approached to assist in securing a ship, but he was such a noted Royalist in those parts that he feared only to bring suspicion on his master by employing himself in such a matter. Instead therefore, he sent Charles '300 broad pieces', which were a most welcome gift, and Wyndham took the business of finding a ship upon himself, going to Lyme for the purpose.

His efforts were successful and it was arranged through a Mr. Ellersdon that the vessel should be off Charmouth on the night of September 22nd. A room was booked at the Queen's Arms, and a little play staged to cover the activities of the party. The landlady was told that the room was taken for a gentleman who had stolen a young gentlewoman to marry her. Wilmot played the lover, Miss Juliana Coningsby, who had taken Jane Lane's place, the fair maid, and Charles the latter's servant. The three spent an anxious night, for the vessel failed to put in an appearance and they feared that they had been betrayed. At dawn, Wilmot set off to Bridport where he learned the reason for the breakdown in their plans. Captain Limbry, the master of the craft, possessed a shrewish wife, her suspicions had been aroused by the news of his hurried departure to sea and she had refused to allow him to leave the house on such dangerous business. On his protesting that he must, she had settled the matter by locking him in the cellar for the night.

Both Lyme and Bridport were swarming with Parliamentary troops, but Charles had promised to meet Wilmot in the latter, and nothing would deter him from keeping his appointment. When they rode into the town they found the yard of the best inn in the place filled with soldiers, but Charles, as usual, put a bold face on the matter and dismounting from his horse barged in amongst them. He was sworn at for his rudeness, but laughed the situation off, only to be accosted by the ostler who cried, 'Sure, sir—I know your face,' and at that moment with the Roundheads crowding about him Charles was never in a more desperate situation. He kept his head however, and entering into jovial conversation with the man ascertained that he came from Exeter, 'Why then,' laughed the King, 'I was in service with a gentleman at Exeter—so 'tis there we must have met.'

In these dangerous surroundings Charles passed the night, and the following morning narrowly escaped capture. Wilmot's horse cast a shoe, and the blacksmith's suspicions were aroused when he noticed the others to be of a Midland make. He told his friend, a weaver, who in turn told the local minister. The Roundhead captain was informed, and finding Charles had left the town, set out in hot pursuit.

The weaver meanwhile, agog with curiosity, visited the inn and accosted the unsuspecting landlady. 'Why—how now—it seems you are a maid of honour.' 'What mean you by that?' replied the worthy woman. 'Why,' he retorted, 'Charles Stuart lay last night at your house and kissed you at his departure, so that you cannot be but a maid of honour.' Whereupon she became exceeding wrath and cried, 'If I thought it was the King, as you say it was, I would think the better of my lips all the days of my life, and so get you out of my house, or I'll get those who shall kick you out.' A truly gallant reply which has lived through the mists of nearly three hundred years, a splendid example of the loyalty of the common people.

The Parliamentarians were galloping along the road to Dorchester but they missed Charles by half a mile, for he had turned off towards Broadwindsor. Here he spent another restless night, since a further detachment of Cromwell's troops occupied the inn, and one of their doxies gave birth to an infant on the kitchen table. The following day he was fortunate enough to regain Colonel Wyndham's house and lay hidden at Trent for the best part of another week.

One night during his stay he heard the joy-bells ringing, and saw some bonfires blazing, with excited people dancing round them. On asking the reason for this jubilation he was informed that they were rejoicing at his own death which had just been reported. 'Indeed,' he said with his deliciously sardonic smile, 'Alas—poor people!'

Another ship was secured at Southampton through the assistance of Colonel Phelipps, but once more the King's hopes were doomed to disappointment. After all had been arranged, the vessel was impressed by the Parliamentarians to carry troops to Jersey.

Colonel Wyndham's was now no longer considered safe, since the Roundheads were hot upon the King's trail and searching many houses in the neighbourhood. Among others, they visited that of Sir Hugh Wyndham, the Colonel's uncle, and there 'seized upon a lovely young lady, saying that she was the King disguised in woman's apparel, nor would they let her go till by some rude experiments they had discovered her sex'.

In this extremity Charles said good-bye to Juliana and removed with Colonel Phelipps to the house of a Mrs. Hyde near Salisbury. By moving in this direction he was also gaining ground towards another ship which had now been secured by a Colonel Gounter.

Mrs. Hyde's loyalty got the better of her discretion, for she received the King with such an open demonstration of respect that it was feared the servants would all become aware of his identity. In these circumstances it was thought best that he should appear to leave her house for good next morning, and taking a public farewell of her he spent the day with Phelipps on the slopes of the rolling plain, and among the monoliths at Stonehenge. By night they returned secretly and he spent a further five days under the hospitable roof of Mrs. Hyde.

Then he journeyed to Hambledon in Hampshire, where he lodged with Colonel Gounter's sister, a Mrs. Symons, and her husband, returning very merry from a party, misled at first by Charles' appearance declared that he thought him 'some Roundhead rogue's son'.

The following day the little party arrived at the small seaport of Brighthelmstone, now so well known as Brighton, and pulled up at the 'George'.

Gounter had employed a loyal merchant named Mansel in the matter of the ship, a coal brig, to carry two Royalists from Shoreham to France for £60 down, but without letting him know the identity of the fugitives, yet Mansel recognized the King immediately.

After dinner, Charles was left alone for a moment in the dining-room of the inn, and was standing before the fire when Mr. Smith, the landlord, entered. As he began to clear the table he started a casual conversation, but he was an ex-guardsman and knew the King's face well. Suddenly he seized the King's hand and kissed it, saying, 'May God bless your Majesty—wheresoever you may go.'

Captain Tattersall had also been ignorant as to who his passengers were to be, but he too recognized Charles' features and, falling on his knees, vowed to venture all that he possessed to set the King and Wilmot safely on the shores of France.

Thus after forty-three days and nights, many of which had been passed in cold and hunger and the whole in an imminent risk of capture, the King was safely conveyed out of the power of his enemies. That he escaped was very largely owing to his own wise decision in the first place not to join Leslie, together with his unfailing wit and bravery, but it was even more largely due to the loyalty and devotion of his subjects. If one includes the servants in the many houses where he rested, there must have been close on a hundred persons in the secret of his identity, and to the poorer of these the reward offered for his capture would have meant ease and plenty all their lives long. Yet there is not a single instance of any one of them endeavouring to betray their King.

The epic closes with a fair wind, and the rising sun gilding the sails of the tall ship as it stands out to sea—and we may be certain that when the news of Charles' safe arrival at Fécamp was spread abroad, many a dust-encrusted bottle was opened and many a cup of good ale drawn, that stout hearts in England might drink—'A Health unto His Majesty'.

THREE

The Making of a Cynic

ARRIVED in France, his 'miraculous preservation' was a nine days' wonder. The Court came out before the gates of Paris to welcome him, and pressed for a recital of his adventures, but Charles would only shake his close-cropped head; nothing would induce him to compromise those friends who had proved so loyal in his hour of need.

The excitement died away and the King was faced with stark reality. He was an exile once more, the unwelcome guest of a power upon whose hospitality he could hardly count from week to week, his pockets empty, and even his mother, at their first supper together on the night of his return, told him that he must pay for his board at her table, beginning with that evening.

Hyde rejoined him, and as Chancellor of a hypothetical Exchequer, entered into a tireless correspondence with every party, state, and person likely to aid the broken fortunes of his master. Hyde's task was no easy one, for he was faced with jealousies and difficulties on every side; Presbyterian oligarchs and Catholic fanatics alike tried to intrigue the King into dangerous understandings, but Charles' faith in his Minister was never shaken, and through the long years the Chancellor, English and Anglican to the backbone, stuck doggedly to the policy of his first declaration that, 'It must be the resurrection of English courage and loyalty that alone should recover England for the King'.

Ormonde, that splendid loyalist, ever filled with generous common sense, and a man after Charles' own heart, was also with him, and Bristol, erratic, uncertain, but enthusiastic. Henry Bennet, later to become Earl of Arlington, and the King's best friend, was despatched on an embassy to Spain, but Wilmot and Jermyn remained in Paris, the former bluff and downright, aching to draw his sword again, the latter, sleek and pompous, the only prosperous member of the party, head of the Queen Mother Henrietta's household, and many said, her lover.

That winter the Court of France was faced with its own troubles. The young King Louis had to be smuggled out of a rebellious Paris to St. Germains, from whence he conducted a war upon his haughty nobles, the leaders of the Fronde. Charles was left destitute in Paris and forced to secure his meals on credit at a tavern, yet despite his privations he kept cheerful—heartening and encouraging his down-at-heels retainers so that the gay Lord Taaffe said of him, 'May I never drink wine if I had not rather live at six *sous* a day with him, than have all the blessings of this world without him.'

Threadbare and penniless he might be, but nothing could rob him of his power to derive joy from simple things, a christening, a dog fight, a good bottle of wine, and a perpetual delight in the conversation of every variety of human being. In addition there were plenty of fair ladies who were happy to have this handsome and amusing young man as their lover for his charm alone. Lady Byron is mentioned about this time as his seventeenth mistress, yet for policy's sake he entered upon more serious affairs, and at his mother's behest paid court to the greatest heiress in France, 'La Grande Mademoiselle'. This fiery and high-nosed princess would have none of him, however, and set her cap at higher game in the person of the young Louis, whereupon Charles, to his intense relief, became free to more than console himself with her lovely maid of honour, the Duchesse de Châtillon.

In '53, the hopes of the Royalists rose with a sudden bound at the news of Cromwell's forcible ejection of the Rump, but nothing came of it. A jester chalked upon the ancient doors at Westminster, 'This House to Let Unfurnished', and the Usurper, setting himself up in the place of Parliament, became more absolute master of Britain than before.

In '54, Charles escaped from his ever-mounting debts in Paris to the friendly city of Cologne, but while he danced to German fiddles or took his exercise upon the ramparts, the industrious Hyde ever kept him informed of all affairs in England.

Then in '55, it seemed that the turn of the tide had really come. Cromwell had declared that all Christians were to be suffered except 'Papists, Prelatists, and teachers of Lewdness', yet the last, like the charge of 'Conduct Unbecoming' against an officer in the Army, could be made to serve a very great variety of purposes. The Churches were put up to let, the Cathedrals ordered to be pulled down, and while the hammers of the Puritans smashed the lovely old stained glass, the sickles of the tax-gatherers cut to the financial roots of the country, ham-stringing commerce and agriculture alike to provide for the upkeep of the ferocious Army.

England was ripe for an attempt to throw off the yoke. Wilmot was sent secretly to London, Ormonde declared himself 'ready to try for a hanging'. By night and day swift couriers sped between the waiting exiles and their friends at home.

In February, Cromwell's spies reported Charles' sudden disappearance from Cologne, and only after weeks of anxious search found him again pacing the sand-dunes of Middleburg, straining his eyes across the sea, and ready instantly to act upon the message that should bid him to start on another attempt to regain his throne.

The message never came. Cromwell's agent, tireless and

ubiquitous, enabled him to arrest the ringleaders and forestall the Royalist plans. Colonel Penruddock alone was able to raise his followers in Wiltshire, and he was speedily defeated. England was divided into ten Military Districts, each with a major-general. Royalist suspects and sympathizers were arrested by the score and transported for life to the slavery of the plantations. Charles, downcast and penniless, retraced his steps to Cologne.

The English Government was now at war with Spain, and in the hope of deriving assistance from the Grandees, Charles went to Brussels, where he placed the swords of himself and his followers at their disposal, early in '56. The gesture resulted in a bitter humiliation, since the proud Spaniards ignored his offer and, with courteous insolence, refused him aid in his destitution.

Charles' next resting-place was the beautiful old town of Bruges, and there may still be seen the gold-mounted bow and arrows with which he used to while away the tedious hours, waiting—for ever waiting, good news out of England. Now again the exile's hopes were high. Cromwell was ruling with such fierce autocracy that even large sections of the Puritans were turning against him. The Levellers, once a powerful party among the Zealots, were now in favour of the King's return. Reams of paper were covered in a correspondence to arrange a rising, but they were moneyless and so was he, the months dragged on, and at last this hope also had to be abandoned.

Bristol now added astrology to his other whimsies, and so intrigued the superstitious Don John of Austria, the Spanish Governor of the Netherlands, that he managed to wring money from his pockets and an official alliance for the King. James, Duke of York, was recalled from his service with the French, where he had proved himself a capable lieutenant to the great Turenne, and sent with his troops to fight against his old commander. Yet this development only served to plunge Charles into greater difficulties than before. The French, quite naturally, stopped his miserable pension. The Spaniards could not bring themselves to offer a sum 'worthy of his acceptance', and the wretched Charles was called upon to support an out-of-elbows army which grew by leaps and bounds owing to the constant stream of fugitives from England.

By '57 the King was in a desperate state. Meat, drink, firing, candles for the past winter, all entirely owed for, but permission was at last received from the Spaniards for him to join his Army at Dunkirk, and there, with James for company, he busied himself with the war against the French. The year was enlivened by the Levellers' unsuccessful attempt against Cromwell's life, and the retaliation by the Lord Protector's spies, who endeavoured to lure the Royal Brothers to an English port, that they might be shot.

At home, things were going from bad to worse. Cromwell's victory had proved his Waterloo. He had made the

Army but he could not shake it off and the land groaned under its tyranny. No less than 12,000 persons were in prison for political offences, but with every arrest there followed fresh outbursts of discontent. The exiles waited, starving but ever hopeful that next week—next month, would bring the joyful news that England had at last revolted from the thraldom of the fanatics.

Buckingham, weary of exile, had made friends with the mammon of unrighteousness. The Parliamentary General, Lord Fairfax, had secured the best part of the Duke's estates as his share of the plunder, so Buckingham went home and married the General's daughter to get his own back. Cromwell put him in the Tower for his pains, but it was another blow for Charles who so greatly enjoyed this versatile rogue's company.

The King spent the summer in Brussels, moving to Hoogstraeten on the Dutch-Flemish frontier in August. During the following months he made frequent excursions into Holland, and there fell deeply in love with Henrietta, the charming daughter of the Dowager Princess of Orange. Henrietta was kind, but the Dowager had no use for 'Charles Lackland' as a son-in-law, and so once more the future King of England drank the cup of humiliation—made the more bitter by disappointment in a genuine love affair.

On his last visit to the lady of his love . . . narrowly escaped capture. An old gentleman s. . . . d him at his inn, secured entrance to his room and locked the door behind him, then flinging off his disguise, he fell upon his knees and begged the King to fly instantly. It was Downing, Cromwell's ambassador to Holland, who had received orders to arrest him if he set foot on Dutch soil, but it was the arch-enemy's last throw. A month later the Great Protector lay dead, worn out from his long struggle with that hydra-headed monster that he had done so much to bring into being.

When the news reached Flanders every Royalist heart flamed with new hope, now at last the great home-coming was a certainty—but it was not to be. Week followed week, no tidings came, the Puritan Army had England by the throat. Winter closed down once more upon the ragged exiles, as they slunk starving to their freezing lodgings in the back streets of the Continental towns.

In '59 Lambert endeavoured to play Cromwell's part. He had the brutality but not the strength, and hopes for the King began to grow again. 'The Sealed Knot', that mysterious society which determined the secret policy of the Royalists, became exceedingly active. Risings were planned to take place in a dozen counties, and the exiles repolished their rusty weapons with grim delight in the work that was to come. Charles hastened to Calais, that he might be ready instantly to embark, then came the terrible news from Samuel Moreland that Sir Richard Willis, who [illegible] high in the councils of the Sealed Knot, had betrayed them. It was too late to countermand the orders in the furthest countries, and before the loyalists in the north, who had risen for the King, had time to concentrate, they were surrounded, outnumbered and destroyed. Again a wave of persecution and arrest laid low the gentry of the English countryside.

Sadly and bitterly Charles turned his steps towards the Pyrenees. France and Spain had now agreed a peace which was to be sealed by the young King Louis' marriage to the Infanta Maria. From that resplendent concourse of Fuenterrabia where the wealth of two great nations was gathered for the ceremony, the luckless, threadbare Prince hoped to beg a few hundred crowns to keep his needy followers from starvation. He even offered to marry the *nouveau riche* heiress Hortense Mancini in his dire necessity, but the wily Mazarin rejected this poor suitor for his niece's hand, declaring hypocritically that 'it was too great an honour', and kept a hold upon his moneybags.

One ray of sunshine lit the King's return. At Colombes he broke his journey to visit his mother, and there, when every hand in Europe was against him, he found fresh encouragement in the love and admiration of his little sister, Henrietta, or Minette, as he called her. She was then only fifteen, but wise beyond her years from a similar adversity to his own, and nothing would persuade her that he was not the greatest, bravest, truest Prince in all the world. Charles, with quick appreciation of her sympathy, opened to her secrets which he would never disclose to his most trusted councillors, his most passionate loves, or any other member of his family. Thus in those few brief days was born a spiritual affection between the two, which lasted till her death, and which no other joy could ever replace in his existence.

Back in Brussels once more, he found Hyde and the rest, up to their eyes in debt, miserable and dejected, yet it seemed that the finding of Minette was a presage of better days to come.

In England, Lambert was quarrelling with the Army, and the Army with the 'Rump'. The tax-gatherers had sucked the last halfpenny from the people, and the troops were mutinous from lack of pay. An angry populace of every sect and party clamoured with ever-growing insistence for the election of a 'Free Parliament' and the salvation from this state of anarchy. As the troubled weeks went by, the eyes of all men gradually centred upon one figure, the strong, taciturn Commander of the well-disciplined Scottish Army, General Monk.

With sudden decision Monk acted. He secured the strong places throughout Scotland, disarmed his Anabaptist officers, and on January 1st, 1660, in the bitter cold of a northern winter, crossed the border into England.

Anxiously, all Europe watched and waited. What did

he mean to do? The exiles' disappointments had been so many and so bitter throughout these long years of hope deferred, they feared that he would only prove another Cromwell. Then with beating hearts they learned that the veteran Fairfax had left his bed to join him, and all Yorkshire risen at his call.

Slowly but steadily Monk's columns wound their way over snow-covered hill and dale, and as they advanced all resistance melted away before them. Yet on the long march southward, he would say no word as to his intentions, and when at last they came over Hampstead hills to London, he was still ominously silent.

A decision by the Aldermen to pay no taxes until a 'Free Parliament' should be called, gave the 'Rump' an opportunty to test Monk's loyalty to themselves. They ordered him to occupy the City. Amidst a tense, watchful silence, he obeyed. Then he assembled his officers, spoke to them of their duty as he saw it, and declared for a 'Free Parliament'. Instantly London and the country were seized with a delirium of joy—yet Monk continued stubbornly silent regarding the Royalists abroad.

On March 16th, the 'Long' Parliament brought its existence to an end by the votes of its excluded members, and at last Monk signified his willingness to receive Sir John Grenville, the Royal emissary. On the 30th Grenville reached Brussels and delivered Monk's message, urging the King to leave the territory of a state with whom England was still at war. Before the Spaniards had time to stop him, Charles galloped across the Dutch frontier and entered Breda.

Here he signed the famous Declaration, agreeing to: A General Amnesty—Security of Tenure for property gained during the late troublous times—Liberty of Conscience—and Arrears of pay for the Army, all as a Free Parliament should determine. With it he sent letters for both Houses and a commission for Monk as Captain General of his Forces.

In April, Lambert escaped from the Tower, but was defeated at Daventry. On the 25th the new Parliament met, and three days later Grenville laid the King's letter before them. They listened to it bareheaded and in silence, then William Morrice moved that the Constitution of England had ever lain—in King—Lords—and Commons. His motion was carried without a dissentient vote. Unanimously the Houses asked that the King should return at once to rule them—then the floodgates of joy were opened, and the House broke up in a pandemonium of wild, tumultuous loyalty.

They knew, as England knew, that the King alone was capable of restoring the good old times, when men were free and money plentiful. They had suffered the tyranny of democracy too long, and the whole nation was shaker with a great, glad happiness at the tidings of his return.

The exiles still hardly dared to believe it true, until a

deputation from the States General arrived, inviting the King to the Hague, and offering the almost unbelievable sum of £30,000 for his expenses. When they reached the Hague they were hardly left time to wonder. By every boat and every road, Loyalists came pouring into the town. From Antwerp, Brussels, Havre, Caen, Paris, Cologne, Rouen, crowding about the Royal lodgings, their faces lit with happiness. Old enemies arrived from England, protesting that they had ever been the King's best friends. The Citizens of London who had howled for the blood of the martyred King sent smiling representatives with £10,000 in gold. Charles had to take his brothers to handle it, because none of them had ever seen so much before.

On May 15th, the Fleet arrived, under Sir Edward Montagu. With him he brought a poor relation, young Samuel Pepys, who on the first day of that year had begun to keep the secret diary which has added so greatly to our knowledge of the period. Healths were drunk, cannon fired and joy bells rung, as on the 22nd Charles went aboard the flagship *Naseby*, now rechristened *Royal Charles*. Anchor was weighed with fifty thousand cheering people on the shore, and the 25th found him at Dover welcomed by the deafening huzzas of fifty thousand more.

The King kissed Monk, who was there to receive him on the beach, calling him 'father' and 'preserver of the crown', then accepting a gilded Bible from the Mayor, declaring it to be 'the thing he loved above all others in the world'. Wild with excitement, half the population of Kent ran cheering and shouting beside his coach to Canterbury, and so, amidst similar scenes of unparalleled enthusiasm, he made his way towards the capital.

On the 29th day of May he entered London, and never was there such a home-coming in the life of any man before or since. The people wept for very joy to see him, their own 'Black Boy', tall, slim, bareheaded, smiling—bowing to either side as he rode through their midst, half deafened by the unceasing plaudits of the multitude. The fountains ran wine, the church bells pealed, the cannon thundered, while thousands upon thousands stood packed in the narrow streets to see him pass. Hoarse with cheering, drunk with joy, wildly elated by the thought that in his person Merrie England was come back once more.

Tired but still smiling, he reached the old Palace of Whitehall, which the homely Mrs. Monk had made ready against his coming. Night drew on, and in every village throughout England the crowds danced round the blazing bonfires delirious with joy. In London the crowd surged hundreds deep about the Palace, yet still the King would not deny the crush that pressed to kiss his hand.

So on his thirtieth birthday he was restored to sovereignty, yet he was of a wisdom far beyond his years, for nearly half his life he had lived abroad in poverty. He knew Frenchmen, Spaniards, Germans, Dutch, the English, Scots and Irish too—princes, peasants, merchants, soldiers, clergy, spies, for he had met and spoken with them all. He knew them for what they were worth and judged them in accordance, remembered their splendid loyalties but forgot not their betrayals. And thus, too sweet natured to bear rancour for past ills, but armed with the bitter knowledge gained during fourteen years in the hard school of adversity, at long last 'The King came into his own again'.

FOUR

The Heady Wine of Great Inheritance

TO APPRECIATE the life of Charles in the years immediately succeeding the Restoration, it is necessary to visualize the age and circumstances of the people who formed his court.

One must banish the memory of those portraits by Lely and Kneller, delineating the heavy-jowled, middle-aged men, and the ripe over-fleshed beauties of a later period; cast aside the weighty periwigs and look beneath the stiff ornate garments of brocade and satin. Then with a clearer eye one can gather some understanding of the hot-blooded, tumultuous youth that thronged the tapestried galleries and gilded chambers of Whitehall.

It was essentially, and above all things, the Court of Youth. The King himself was just 30, and his brother James, Duke of York, who as his heir was the next most important person in the Kingdom, was 27.

The gorgeous, scatterbrained Duke of Buckingham was 32, and those Earls who were the constant companions of the King, Ossary, Falmouth, Dorset, Arran, and Sunderland, 26, 24, 22, 21 and 20 respectively. While Rochester, who more than any, in his triple capacity of great noble, drunken debauché, and man of letters, epitomizes the courtier of the period, was only 17 when he became a leading figure at the Court.

In addition to these gay young lords who held position near the King by right of birth, Charles delighted to have about him that brilliant band of rapscallions who contributed so much to the wit and literature of the age—Dryden, Etheridge, Jermyn, Montagu, Sedley, and Wycherley, whose ages at the Restoration were 29, 26, 24, 24, 21, and 20—all, therefore, in the first vigour of their youth.

The women, too, were of an even more tender age—most of them being no more than slips of girls in the first flush of their beauty, when they entered upon that riot of intrigue, without which it is doubtful if their names would have come down to posterity.

To the natural exuberance of youth must be added the heady wine of great inheritance. It was not possible for Charles to restore every cavalier to his estates—to have done so would have caused immediate revolution—but large numbers did regain their patrimony, and to those who participated in his exile or assisted in his escape after Worcester he scattered with a lavish hand all the benefits which he was able. Lordships of the Bed Chamber, Groomships, and Governances, all of which carried considerable emoluments. The needy band who a few years before had been hard put to it to secure a crust at the King's impoverished table, or in foreign universities had anxiously awaited the questionable arrival of remittances from England, now found the pockets of their new silk breeches bursting with golden guineas.

Above all, the war was over, and these people who from their early youth had known danger, hardship, uncertanty and distress, had at last come home, freed from the clutches of foreign landladies, welcomed and restored, safe once more to ride the broad acres without fear of death, imprisonment or fine—and all in the glory of an English summer.

In our own day we have known the reaction that followed upon those years of horror, when every able-bodied man received the Armistice as a reprieve from certain death or mutilation. We know that as a result of the strain which the nation had undergone, there was an epidemic of free love, and a sudden uprush of talent among the younger generation. In the pyjama and bottle parties, the night clubs, and the doings of the 'bright young people' of the early 1920s we see reflected the licence of the Restoration, and in the writings of Huxley, Coward, Joyce, Sassoon, Lawrence, to name but a few, a repetition of the flame that lit the 1660s. The King himself was young, generous, elegant, and witty, it was therefore but to be expected that the hectic gaiety natural to the circumstances of his contemporaries should centre about his person.

During the months that followed the Restoration every highway throughout the length and breadth of England was gay with cavalcades. Clumsy windowless coaches bumped and jolted over the miles of grassy ruts, Churchmen upon docile mules, and ladies riding pillion, laughing horsemen galloping upon the springy turf—one and all wending their way through shady forest or over rolling down towards the magic centre of Whitehall—to see the King, to kiss his hand; and if he was, from sheer lack of funds and posts, unable to grant every favour that they asked, at least he ordered that none, however humble, should be turned away, and pledged his credit, that he might recognize their loyalty by invitations to a long series of splendid entertainments.

By the end of October the Queen Mother was back in England, and with her, to conquer every heart, came Minette. Buckingham fell desperately in love with her, and to pleasure this dear sister there was nothing in the world to which Charles would not agree. A fresh round of gaieties was initiated in her honour, and the King, fretting at the ties of state which kept him from her when she went to Tunbridge Wells, slips a pressing note to the faithful Hyde, now Earl of Clarendon, 'I would willingly make a visit to my sister—when can I find the time?' 'I suppose,' replies the ponderous minister, 'your Majesty will go with a light train.' 'I intend to take nothing but my night bag,' cries the King. 'But surely,' protests Clarendon, 'you will not travel without forty or fifty horse.' 'I count that part of my night bag,' laughs the impatient Charles.

No sooner had the festivities attendant on the triumphant homecoming died down, than the Coronation was ordered for the following spring. It was celebrated in April with a blaze of Royal Pageantry and accompanied by a renewed burst of gaiety in which the whole Kingdom once again participated.

Then a marriage was arranged. Little Catherine of Braganza arrived at Portsmouth in May of 1662, bringing as her dowry half a million pounds, Tangier, and Bombay—and in her train some very unprepossessing Maids of Honour, some very dirty monks and—a curiously oriental attendant for a woman—a barber skilled in the art of depilation!

Catherine was a dowdy little person, her legs too short, her body too long, but her face was redeemed by a pair of large, soft, dark eyes. She had been brought up with the greatest strictness, and all knowledge of the world kept from her; she suffered, therefore, in proportion to her ignorance when she became aware of the custom of the age, by which all crowned heads married from policy, and kept a series of mistresses for their amusement.

That she loved the tall, dark King to the end of his

days is a testimony to his unfailing kindness and thought for her—but being human, more he could not give. After a little she resigned herself to his infidelities, comforted herself with innumerable dishes of tea, and learned to alternate her pious devotions with participation in the gaieties of the Court—gaining by the latter the approbation of her husband, and much genuine pleasure for herself.

Of those ladies who caused the Queen so many jealous, unhappy tears during her first months in England, Barbara Villiers was the most prominent. As Mrs. Palmer she had already become intimate with Charles at the Hague, and Palmer, upon the Restoration, was created Earl of Castlemaine; yet he quarrelled with the King, not, as might be supposed, about his wife, but on religious questions, and, being an ardent Catholic, took himself off to act as Chamberlain to the Pope, Barbara thereon becoming the open and undisputed Queen of Whitehall.

A dark-haired, blue-eyed beauty of imperious temperament, she remained Charles' mistress for the best part of twelve years, and a powerful entity at Court until his death. That she was very lovely there can be no doubt, and Pepys was one of the many who paid tribute to her attractions by unruly prickings of the flesh whenever he saw her at the theatre or about the Court, yet it is difficult to understand the secret of her lasting fascination for the King. No single writer on the period has a good word to say in her defence. She was consistently unfaithful to Charles, yet shrewishly jealous of his infidelities to her, avaricious to a degree and possessing the temper of a virago. The latter characteristic alone one would have thought sufficient speedily to sicken the indolent, peace-loving monarch, yet by some mysterious means she kept her place and a certain hold on his affections. If one may use the expression 'bed-worthy', Barbara, in common with all really great courtesans, seems to have possessed that attribute in a very high degree, and Charles may have forgiven her much on this account. Good-natured people are also more than usually liable to allow their affections to become a habit, and the King, who was the kindest of men, was doubtless loath to cast aside one from whom he had derived so much pleasure.

Castlemaine was by no means a fool for all her tantrums, and materially assisted the prolongation of her reign by a political alliance with Buckingham, Arlington, and the rest of the anti-Clarendonian party. Moreover, when the King's first passion for her had worn off, and in order to cover her own affair with the spindle-legged Harry Jermyn, she adopted the policy by which Madame de Pompadour later kept Louis XV enslaved for so many years—the production of other, more temporary, occupants for the Royal bed; young women of undoubted physical attractions but insufficient brain to threaten her own supremacy.

The most famous of these was a Miss Frances Stewart, who had lately been a Maid of Honour at the Court of France, and returned to England in the Queen Mother's train. 'La Belle Stewart' was a tall, slender girl of surpassing beauty, but so little brain as to be almost an idiot. Her favourite recreations were building card houses and playing blind man's buff; she had, however, acquired in France a very excellent taste in dress which was universally admired by both women and men.

Castlemaine took this nymph under her wing, and moreover into her bed, so that Charles might joke with them both together when he paid his morning call, and very soon he was desperately smitten with this little Roman-nosed piece of nonsense.

The Queen at this juncture fell desperately ill, and for some time her life was despaired of. For two nights her Portuguese attendants, by continuous prayer and chanting, kept her from all hope of sleep, and on the third, Charles proved that however much he might be in love with another woman he was none the less a devoted husband. He summoned his own physicians, flung out the priests and danglers of precious relics neck and crop, aired the rooms, and commanded silence in the corridors; then, kneeling at her bedside, he prayed her, with tears in his eyes, to live for his sake. She wept to see him cry, but took courage from his affection, and after a long illness, during which he was her constant attendant, pulled through. Catherine had already found that life at the Court of this pleasant, kindly Prince was far more agreeable than in a Portuguese convent, and on her recovery this devout Catholic woman rebutted the suggestion of her almoner that a cup of holy bones had saved her by the reply that 'she owed her life to her husband's prayers'.

Frances Stewart meanwhile proved stubborn. Whether it was due to a true innocence natural in her sixteen years —but very strange in any friend of Castlemaine's—or a calculated resistance in the hope that Catherine would die and she be made Queen, is doubtful, but in any case the amorous monarch met with little success. He pursued her into corners upon every possible occasion, and even paid her the compliment of having her fair form stamped upon his coinage, where it may be seen in the image of Britannia to the present day, but the minx would never yield him the least favour.

So enamoured of her was Charles that his passion even brought forth a latent literary ability in this many-gifted Prince.

> 'I pass all my hours in a shady old grove,
> But I live not the day when I see not my love;
> I survey every walk now my Phillis is gone,
> And sigh when I think we were there all alone,
>   O then, 'tis O then, that I think there's no hell,
>   Like loving, like loving too well.

While alone to myself I repeat all her charms,
She I love may be locked in another man's arms,
She may laugh at my cares and so false she may be
To say all the kind things she before said to me.
O then, 'tis O then, that I think there's no hell,
Like loving too well.

But when I consider the truth of her heart,
Such an innocent passion, so kind without art;
I fear I have wronged her, and hope she may be
So full of true love to be jealous of me:
And then, 'tis I think that no joys be above
The pleasures of love.'

And who that has ever loved cannot find their own feelings reproduced in the stanzas of this very human King. The fears expressed in the second verse of the song were to be realized only too soon. Castlemaine, becoming jealous of her protégée, took Charles on a surprise visit to the young lady's bedroom, when she had pleaded illness as an excuse for keeping to her room—and there, seated on her bed, was the Duke of Richmond. The King was furious; he had paid her such very marked attention, and, lenient as he was by nature, he deeply resented being made to look a fool in public. He blazed out at the unfortunate Richmond, who mildly replied that, after all, he was prepared to marry the girl, which was more than the King could do, but for once Charles' sense of humour failed to respond to a joke against himself. Cut to the quick, he gave way for once to an outburst of real temper, dismissing the Duke, with a torrent of abuse, from the bedroom and his Court.

The matter did not end thus, however. Richmond returned secretly one night to Whitehall and, under cover of darkness and a violent storm, abducted the lady from under the King's very nose. Together the lovers fled on horseback to the country, and were married the next day. Once more the King had difficulty in restraining his anger, but later he had his own back, for on her return to Court, the beautiful Duchess of Richmond freely accorded him those favours as a wife which she had denied him as a maid.

That his outburst in Frances Stewart's bedroom was contrary to his nature is shown by his treatment of Mrs. Roberts, who also for some time had been one of his mistresses. This lady deceived him in order to satisfy the ardour of the tempestuous Rochester. When her infidelity was discovered, she sorely wished to regain the King's affections, and, seeing him pass down the corridor one morning when she was dressing, she rushed out of her bedroom with her lovely hair all in disorder and, flinging herself at his feet, implored pardon for her frailty. Charles, overcome by these simulated agonies, raised her up, took her in his arms and protested that 'no man could see her and not love her'. Then he waited upon her in her lodgings, where the reconciliation was completed.

That he was apt to wander through all parts of the Palace we see from the episode of his pausing one morning opposite the apartments of the Maids of Honour, his attention caught by the treble rendering of an exceedingly lewd song about himself, in which he was compared to his lusty stallion, 'Old Rowley'. He knocked upon the door. 'Who's there?' came the voice of Mrs. Howard, the mistress of the Maids. ' 'Tis Old Rowley himself, ma'am,' replied Charles, with a smile, as he poked his nose round the crack of the door.

Other mistresses there were who held the Royal favour for a little time, and others again who in after years played an important part, but of these we shall speak later.

The Duke of York had also married, and that within four months of the Restoration. In Holland he had conceived a wild passion for Anne Hyde, Clarendon's daughter. As heir to the throne, it was his duty to consult the King, and in due course to submit to a foreign alliance for the benefit of the country—but he married Anne in secret. The following morning he fell upon his knees before his brother and broke the news in a flood of tears. Charles was naturally upset, but he sent for two of his oldest and most trusted counsellors, Ormonde and Southampton, and asked them to tell the lady's father as tactfully as possible—but Hyde was furious. He declared that he would rather see his daughter the Duke's whore than his wife, and suggested cutting off her head as the speediest way of annulling the marriage. Malicious gossip was spread about that Anne had had a number of lovers, and James weakly allowed himself to be persuaded into a scheme for disowning her, but Charles refused to listen to these slanders. His attitude throughout this sordid affair shows the true nobility of his character. He told his brother with great kindness that, now the thing was done, they must needs make the best of it; reassured his old minister of his conviction that this was no plot whereby he had sought advancement for his family, and forced him to accept an Earldom and a grant of £20,000 as a mark of his respect—then went at once to visit the unfortunate Anne, already lying in with her first baby, and embraced her as a sister with the greatest tenderness.

Few women could have supported her new position as Duchess of York better than Anne Hyde. She was a tall girl, with a good figure and naturally majestic air; she was also possessed of considerable wit, but the fact that hers was a love-match did not save her from the same troubles as the Queen. James was consistently unfaithful to her; in fact, it seems that he made a habit of endeavouring to seduce his wife's Maids of Honour.

In Miss Jennings, the beautiful cendré blonde with the generous mouth and lovely features, he caught a tartar, since not only did she repulse his advances but used deliberately to let his love letters drop out of her muff in the most crowded assemblies for all and sundry to pick up and read. Neither was he more successful with the beautiful Lady Chesterfield. Her husband, noticing that the Duke's hand had disappeared under his lady's skirts when seated next her one night at cards in the Queen's chamber, rushed her off to the country before further harm could befall her, despite the fact that the incident occurred in the depths of winter.

With Lady Denham he was more fortunate. She was a relative of the restless and ambitious Earl of Bristol, who endeavoured to arrange for her to become mistress to the King in the hope of being able to use her for political ends. The lady's attractions proved insufficient to ensnare Charles; she was passed on to James, but his happiness was short-lived. Her husband learnt of the affair and brought it to a premature conclusion by poisoning the poor lady with an infusion in chocolate.

The notorious Lady Southesk then attracted James' attention and proved an easy conquest, but with his usual hole-in-the-corner methods he would not compromise himself by visiting her house alone, and that excess of caution brought about his undoing. On one occasion he took Richard Talbot to keep him in countenance, and Talbot, lately returned out of Portugal, was not *au courant* with the latest news at Court. York retired with the lady and Talbot was left to kick his heels in the drawing-room, where, leaning from a window, he saw a coach drive up to the house, and a familiar figure alight. 'Hullo, Carnegie,' he cried. 'Welcome my good fellow, where the devil have you been since we were at Brussels together, and what the deuce has brought you here? Do you also want to see Lady Southesk? If you do, my poor friend, you had better go and seek a mistress elsewhere, for I don't mind telling you in confidence that the Duke of York is in love with her, and as a matter of fact he is with her in her bedroom at this very moment.' To Talbot's surprise, Carnegie went purple in the face with rage, stood silent for a moment, and then—shaking his fist angrily at the house—leapt back into his coach again. When James returned from the lady's embraces, Talbot told him of this strange encounter. 'Thou fool,' stormed James. 'Dost thou not know that old Southesk is dead, and that Carnegie hath inherited his title?'

Returning to his wife's Maids of Honour, James then fixed his affections on Miss Arabella Churchill, whose brother was later to become the famous Duke of Marlborough. This affair was of a more lasting nature and by her he had three children—James, Duke of Brunswick, Henry, Duke of Albemarle, and Henrietta, Lady Walgrave. She was a clever creature, but exceptionally plain; tall, pale-faced, and pimply, with a body that was nothing but skin and bones—but James' mistresses were always notoriously unattractive, which once caused Charles to remark, with his languid smile, 'Odd's fish! I do believe 'tis my brother's Confessor who chooses his mistresses for him—by way of penance.'

Poor James was by no means a happy young man, since that Confessor played a considerable part in his existence, and his earnest religious faith was at continual war with those instincts which urged him to tiptoe along the corridor where slept the Maids of Honour. He was sincere and candid, but lacking altogether his brother's humour and quick intelligence. It was Buckingham who said of the two, 'Charles could see things if he would—James would see things if he could.' In Council he always urged the exercise of the prerogative to its utmost limits, advice to which Charles was far too wise to listen, and a policy which, coupled with his religious fervour, later cost him his throne. But despite his narrow, bigoted outlook and rather mean, haughty disposition, he did really good work in a conscientious, plodding way for the Navy, during his time as Lord High Admiral.

Owing to the Coronation and the King's marriage, the festivities which had begun with the Restoration stretched well into the third year of Charles' actual reign. Balls, masques, and parties of pleasure on the river were the established order of the day, and every kind of frolic was entered into with the greatest zest.

Buckingham, who was more fitted for the post of

Court Jester than a great lord, led the revels. His hospitality was royal, his dress magnificent, and he moved so gracefully that it was impossible not to follow him with the eye as he walked down the crowded galleries. Something of his mercurial nature and ever-changing tastes are shown in the following verse:

> 'Everything by starts and nothing long,
> But, in the course of one revolving moon,
> Was Chemist, Fiddler, Statesman, and Buffoon,
> Then all for Women, Painting, Rhyming, Drinking,
> Besides a thousand freaks that died in thinking.'

So perfect a mimic was he that Charles almost died of laughing to see him pass in mock state through the Royal Apartments, with pursed lips and puckered brows, seemingly overwhelmed with the cares of office, a pair of bellows hanging before him to imitate the Purse, and preceded by Colonel Titus, bearing a shovel in place of the Mace—so naturally did he take off the air of Clarendon, the serious-minded Minister.

On another occasion the whole Court rocked with mirth when Lady Muskerry, who was known to be in an interesting condition, appeared in a farthingale, and the cushion falling from under her skirts while dancing Buckingham seized upon it with loud shouts, whipped off his coat, wrapped it about the pillow, and ran wildly up and down the room—mimicking the cries of a new-born babe and shouting, 'A nurse—a nurse for the young Muskerry,' among the Maids of Honour.

Tom Killigrew was actual holder of the title 'Master of the Revels', and it was he who, to the surprise of the beholders, appeared one night at a Court Ball fully booted and spurred as though about to set out immediately on a journey. 'And where are you going at this hour, pray?' asked the King. 'To Hell—may it please your Majesty,' replied Killigrew promptly. 'Odd's fish! what for?' exclaimed the astonished Charles. 'Why, to fetch Oliver Cromwell back, to get the country out of the mess it's in,' cried the audacious jester. The pause must have been quite appalling while the Court watched the face of the King, but Charles loved a jest, and Killigrew, who had begun life as page to Charles I, was permitted much familiarity. The King smiled, the lofty chamber was soon echoing with uproarious laughter, and another night of gaiety at Whitehall had opened with a swing.

Killigrew also held the post of Groom of the Bedchamber, and in May, 1662, succeeded in getting his wife appointed to what sounds an enchanting office, 'Keeper of the Sweet Coffer' to the Queen. The appointment, however, appears to have been somewhat offset by another in the following month, namely, 'First Lady of the Privy'.

More serious work than either Jester or Groom occupied most of Killigrew's time, since he was responsible for the management of 'The King's Company of Actors' performing at Drury Lane. The theatres had reopened immediately upon the Restoration and a second troupe 'The Duke's Company' were soon established under William D'Avernant in Lincoln's Inn, both being freely patronized by Court and City.

Instead of young boys, who always took the female parts before the Civil War, actresses were employed for the first time, and many of these good-looking, high-spirited young women soon found their way to Court, adding their laughter and highly seasoned wit to that of the titled ladies, who were hardly less restrained.

Among them was Moll Davis, who in a play entitled *The Mad Shepherdess* sang a little ditty entitled *My lodging is on the Cold Ground* with such affecting pathos that she very soon changed it for one in a far better place. In fact, she got a ring worth £600, a house in Suffolk Street, and a child by the King christened Mary Tudor, who at the tender age of fourteen married the Earl of Derwentwater.

Charles was a great lover of the theatre and, quite apart from his thoughtful care for such likely lasses as Moll, he was a generous patron to the leading actors of the day—Hart, Betterton, Harris, Mohun, and the rest. He was also a true friend to the dramatists who flourished in his time.

John Dryden, who is now perhaps the best remembered, was appointed Poet Laureate and Royal Historiographer. Among his best plays are *The Indian Emperor, Marriage à la Mode,* and *The Conquest of Granada,* but almost more fame attaches to his name from his political satire *The Hind and the Panther.*

William Wycherley, who had passed his youth in Paris and spent much time among the fashionable literary society of the Hotel Rambouillet, was another. He wrote *Love in a Wood, The Country Wife,* and *The Plain Dealer.* Through the latter, in addition to much applause, he gained a wife, since he met the lady, then the widow of the Earl of Drogheda, in a bookshop at Epsom, purchasing a copy of his own play. He succeeded Harry Jermyn in Castlemaine's affections, but Charles bore him no malice, and valued him so highly that when he fell seriously ill, the King visited him in his Bow Street lodgings and perhaps saved his life by a gift of five hundred guineas which enabled him to make a prolonged convalescence at Montpellier.

Johnny Crowne, a Nova Scotian who came to England early in the reign, was of a lesser talent; a prim but amiable man whom some thought a dull fellow, yet his *Sir Courtley Nice* was still acted a century after his death, and seventeen of his plays were produced in his lifetime.

Shadwell's plays also numbered seventeen, and among them was *Sullen Lovers.* There was also poor Nat Lee, who drank so heavily when he grew older that his mind became affected, and he had to be removed to Bedlam.

Then there were the titled dramatists. Sir George Etheridge, the handsome young exquisite, who like Wycherley had been educated in France, produced three slender but delicious comedies after the manner of Molière—*The Comical Revenge, She Would if She Could,* and *The Man of Mode.*

Sir Charles Sedley, whose first and best known play was *The Mulberry Garden*, so called after that part of the grounds near Buckingham Palace where James I had planted mulberry trees in the hope of introducing the silk-worm to English commerce. It was on the first night of one of Sedley's plays that the roof of the theatre fell in, upon which Sir Fleetwood Sheppard told the author that 'there was so much fire in the piece that it blew up the poet, the audience and the whole building'. 'No,' replied Sedley, quickly, 'on the contrary, the play is so heavy that it has demolished the theatre and buried the author among his own rubbish.' Sedley's claim to fame, however, rests more upon his lyrics than his plays, and, rake-hell and drunkard as he was, he must have had a higher side to produce such enchanting things as this—*To Celia.*

'Not Celia, that I juster am
Or better than the rest;

For I would change each hour with them
Were not my heart at rest.

But I am tied to very thee
But every thought I have:
Thy face I only care to see,
Thy heart I only crave.

All that in women is adored
In thy dear self I find—
For the whole sex can but afford
The handsome and the kind.

Why then should I seek further store
And still make love anew;
When change itself can give no more.
'Tis easy to be true.'

To mention Etheridge and Sedley is to think immediately of Buckhurst, for in the scandalous annals of the period the three formed an inseparable partnership reminiscent of the Musketeers of fiction, with Rochester as an unprincipled edition of D'Artagnan.

Charles Sackville, Lord Buckhurst and later Earl of Dorset, was a young man of exceptional good looks and quite a charming poet. In character he was of a generous, kindly disposition which none of the other three could claim, and if he could not rival them in the quality of his art, he was certainly art's most splendid patron.

To him Wycherley owed the success of his *Plain Dealer*, and it was he who introduced Samuel Butler's *Hudibras* to Whitehall. To him also we owe the beauty of Prior's verse, since later in life he came upon the poet as a poor boy reading a tattered copy of *Horace* in a tavern called 'The Rummers' near Whitehall, and, taking him away, he provided for his future. During the whole of his life he was 'the patron of men of genius, and the dupe of women, and bountiful beyond measure to both', so that it was said of him that 'He furnished Knole with silver, and peopled it with poets and courtesans'.

Unfortunately, Buckhurst suffered from the curious disability of being nearly tongue-tied until mildly drunk. He therefore found it necessary to be in an almost perpetual state of intoxication, and this led him into an unusual number of scrapes. In one instance he set out with four other gay young sparks to accompany a Mr. Vernon on the first stage out of London. On their return they heard at Waltham Cross that there were highwaymen upon the road, and meeting with an unfortunate tanner, they set upon and killed him, in the belief that he was a member of the band. They were promptly arrested and the coroner found it to be 'plain murder'; but luckily the King was ever a good friend in need and, possessing a particular fondness for the young man, he gave instructions that the charge be reduced to 'manslaughter'—or, as Pepys tells us, 'they had all been hanged on the Monday'.

Another hectic party in which Buckhurst was concerned took place at the 'Cock Tavern' in Bow Street, kept by old Oxford Kate, this time with Sir Charles Sedley and Sir Thomas Ogle for companions. With Buckhurst it appears to have been a particularly loquacious evening, which is as good as saying that he was very drunk indeed. So drunk, in fact, were the whole party that they stripped off all their clothes and proceeded to dance round the room stark naked. This would not have mattered greatly, but they needs must perform the same antics upon the first floor balcony in full view of the street, and proceeded to scandalize the assembled multitude by adopting all the most vicious postures in the nude which they could think of. The mob were furious at this indecency, and the roisterers were only rescued from the clutches of the angry crowd, who stormed the tavern, with the greatest difficulty. All London was shocked and offended by this unseemly exhibition, and the lewd jesters were bound over to keep the peace in a sum of £5,000.

John Wilmot, Earl of Rochester, was the son of that great Cavalier who had been the King's companion during the flight after Worcester, and when in 1664 he presented himself at Court, he was naturally given a very kind reception. He was then a thin-faced, fair-haired stripling fresh from his travels in France and Italy and adorned with a natural modesty—which, with his quick intelligence and ready wit, soon won him a foremost place among the King's intimates.

How long he preserved that modesty is not recorded, but his wit is with us still, and as a satirist he holds a high place in English literature. Unfortunately much of his most amusing verse is quite unprintable at the present day, but, on the other hand, many of his poems possess a delicacy of thought and purity of motive which approach sheer beauty. He was capable of writing the most indecent satires in one mood, and, in another, songs of such airy charm as the following:

'I Promis'd Sylvia to be true;
Nay, out of Zeal, I swore it too
And that she might believe me more,
Gave her in writing what I swore;

Not Vows, not Oaths can Lovers bind;
So long as bless'd, so long they're kind:
'Twas in a Leaf, the Wind but blew,
Away both Leaf and Promise flew.'

Rochester soon became one of the most powerful patrons of the drama, and Dryden owed much of his first success to his friendship. Later, however, they quarrelled and the Earl gave his patronage to Settle and

Crowne. In the meantime he had found ample leisure to go the pace with the wildest rakes of Whitehall, and on account of one escapade had been sent to the Tower before he was nineteen.

This affair concerned a Miss Mallet, a beauty of considerable fortune from the north. He fell violently in love with her, and, since her family would not listen to his suit, he took the law into his own hands. The lady was proceeding home one night in her coach, accompanied by her grandfather, when Rochester and his bravoes fell upon them at Charing Cross. The girl was dragged out and placed in another coach which drove off at all speed to Uxbridge, but the abduction was a failure as the family set off in hot pursuit and regained possession of the lady.

It seems that the enchanting Miss Mallet had a number of beaux, and she herself summed up her situation with regard to them in the following neat manner: 'Lord Hinchinbroke was indifferent to have her, Lord John Butler might not have her, Lord Herbert would have her, Sir Francis Popham would do anything to have her, and Lord Rochester would have her by force.' And Rochester did have her, for, although he had to wait two years, he married her in the end.

He was far from being a faithful husband, yet a very real devotion existed between the two, right up till his death. It was his practice to spend each winter at Court and the summer in the country, and he seems to have taken great pleasure in the rural joys of his estates, where life in the bosom of his family was enlivened by his zest for practical jokes. Often he roamed the country disguised as a tramp, and on one occasion visited Burford in the guise of a tinker. There he collected all the pots and pans he could lay his hands on, but instead of mending them he knocked all their bottoms out, for which piece of nonsense the angry villagers clapped him in the stocks. His wit, however, proved equal to the occasion. He sent a note to his steward for his coach, and when it arrived that night, his henchmen dug up stocks, Rochester, and all—and thus conveyed him home.

It was principally during these long sojourns in the country that he composed his scandalous satires against the people at Court, and many were at a loss to know how he procured his uncanny knowledge of their most secret peccadilloes. The truth of the matter was that he had engaged a footman who knew everybody of note by sight, equipped the fellow with a red coat and a musket, and kept him posted every night near the Whitehall lodgings of those about whom he required information. Nobody, of course, suspected a sentry, and Rochester secured first-hand knowledge of all the latest amours.

Charles' own dictum on humour was, 'Good jests should bite like lambs—not dogs; they should cut, not wound,' but Rochester's opinion was very different. Even when his satires were aimed at his best friends he could not restrain his pen from a cruel malice, and his bitter humour earned him many enemies—yet these so feared the lash of further attacks that they dared not quarrel with him openly.

One may perhaps be excused for quoting the opening lines of 'A Satyr' which he one day slipped into the King's pocket, since, although it is by no means so indecent as many of his verses, nothing can so well exemplify the nature of his scurrilous attacks—as this, upon a generous friend and master.

'Preserv'd by wonder in the Oak O Charles
And then brought in by the Duke of Albemarle
The first by Providence, the next all Devil,
Show's thour't a Compound made of Good and Evil—
The Bad we'ave too long known, the Good's to come,
But not expected till the day of Doom;
Was ever Prince's Soul so meanly Poor,
To be a slave to every little Whore?
The Seamans Needle nimbly points the Pole
But thine still turns to every * * * *
* * * * * * * * * * * * * *
* * * * * * * * * * * *
* * * is the Mansion House where thou dost dwell,
But thou art fix'd as Tortoise to her shell,
Whose Head peeps out a little now and then
To take air, and then creeps in again.'

For this witty piece of nastiness he was sent to the Tower, and indeed from the time of his first coming to Court there was rarely a year elapsed when he was not sent upon a similar excursion for the same type of offence. Yet Charles was ever more ready to forgive than punish, and it went against the grain to deprive himself of this amusing companion for long—so Rochester was always speedily set at liberty again.

The Comte de Grammont, that amusing Frenchman who was banished by Louis XIV for looking too amorously at one of his own lady loves, and passed the most agreeable of exiles at the Court of Charles, who adopted him into his innermost circle, once said of Rochester, 'If he could by any means divest himself of one half of his wit, the other would make him the most agreeable man in the world'—and we may assume that it was that second half which so endeared him to the King.

Such, then, were the principal personages, nearly all in their riotous twenties, among whom Charles moved and had his being, during the first decade of his actual kingship, and it must not be imagined that they were only occasional visitors to his Court.

The Palace of Whitehall in those early days was a great rambling mass of buildings, which covered more than a quarter of a million square feet along the bend of the river bank. Between it and the City proper lay three miles of private gardens, open spaces and suburbs; the highway between the two being the splendid waterway of the Thames, which at that time carried such an abundance of colourful traffic that it has been compared to the Grand Canal in Venice. The Palace and its adjacent buildings were as a little town set completely apart, and there were housed not only the Queen and Duchess of York, with their Maids of Honour, but the Mistresses, Ministers, great Officers of State, Courtiers and Soldiers, together with their dependants and retainers.

The King, as the head and virtual father of this vast multitude resembling almost an Oriental family, met them constantly in the galleries and the anti-chambers, or on the river steps and bowling green, with a pleasant word, and kindly thoughtfulness for the welfare of them all.

Upon their lives, therefore, his character must have exercised considerable influence, yet no one can deny that by such constant contact *their* age and circumstances must have had much influence on his own.

FIVE

The Power behind the Throne

FROM the foregoing description of the tastes and morals of Charles' most intimate companions, one might well imagine that the legend of him—as an idle, dissipated Monarch, who allowed the affairs of his Kingdom to go hang—is correct.

That he was dissipated there is no doubt, and we have ample proof that he developed 'the gentle art of idling gracefully' to an apotheosis, but what the historians of our school-days fail to point out is that Charles put in a nineteen-hour day.

Up at five in the morning with the greatest regularity, and rarely in bed before midnight, his magnificent physique enabled him to ride, hunt, shoot, fish, swim, or row upon the river in the early hours of the morning, laze among his courtiers in the evening, indulge his amorous propensities by candle-light—and yet devote the middle hours of the day to business with intelligence and ability.

Rochester once nailed the oft-quoted verse upon his bedroom door:

'Here lies our Sovereign Lord the King,
Whose Promise none relies on;
He never said a Foolish Thing,
Nor ever did a Wise One.'

'That may well be,' replied the Monarch with his quiet, dark smile. 'For my discourse is my own, but my actions are my Ministers'.' Yet in actual fact no statement could be less true.

In European history one often comes across a phrase 'The Power behind the Throne' in application to various influences ranging from the genius of a Cardinal Richelieu to the perfumed breath of a Madame du Barry. In the case of Charles II it was a sort of dual personality. A Second Man with a firm chin and able brain who lurked at the elbow of the amiable, good-natured Monarch, embodying all his finest qualities—that alone was the Power behind the Throne.

With consummate skill he selected the men most appropriate for his Ministers, utilized them to deal with his unruly Parliaments, coaxed and encouraged them to put forward measures which he wished to pass, or gently curbed their impetuosity; so that they acted always in accordance with his will, though often in ignorance of his secret policy, which he pursued with tranquil, undeviating determination.

His first business upon his Restoration was to make

legal the promises which he had given in the Declaration of Breda.

Firstly, he had undertaken that the Standing Army should receive their arrears of pay and be disbanded. For an entire decade it had ruled the country with a ruthless force, subject to no authority but that of its leaders. It was detested by the people who had suffered under an appalling burden of taxation for its upkeep, and Charles was quick to realize how helpless he would be in the face of any sudden opposition from this armed body, drawn from stern Puritan sources. Therefore, by a stupendous financial effort, he raised the money to satisfy their demands, and, with a sigh of thankfulness, saw these 40,000 sober Ironsides lay down their weapons.

At the same time the shrewd King felt that a small body of highly trained, well-armed men who were devoted to his person might prove extremely useful in times of trouble; so he retained Monk's crack regiment, the Coldstream, as household troops, and a cohort of picked cavalry who became known as 'The Blues'. Further, he re-embodied two new regiments whose loyalty could be depended on—'The Royal Scots', from Cavaliers who in exile had taken service under the King of France, and 'The Buffs', from similar adherents who had served under the banner of Holland.

The second question was the granting of a General Amnesty for all who had taken up arms against his father or himself. The only exceptions to this were to be the Regicides who had participated in the trial and execution of Charles I, but upon this question the nation did not show by any means the same unanimity as it had in the disbandment of the Army.

The new Parliament met in January, 1661, and as a result of the tremendous reaction it was Royalist to the backbone. Many of the members were extremely young, but on this being pointed out to the King, he was so delighted by their first demonstration of loyalty that he exclaimed, 'Odd's fish—what matter, I will keep them till they grow beards,' but he soon found that their exuberance took a very dangerous form.

Had he allowed them to have their way, the result would have been appalling—nothing less than a White Terror would have swept through the land, engulfing the old Parliamentarians in a tornado of fines, imprisonment, and death. There was not a country squire in the length and breadth of England but had some insult or persecution to avenge, and the new Cavalier Parliament was packed with their representatives.

Quietly but firmly Charles undertook the difficult task of setting his face against his own most devoted supporters. In vain they accused him of being a bad son forgetful of his father's death, and a false friend who neglected to right the wrongs that they had suffered in his cause. With good-natured remonstrance he quieted their cries for blood and vengeance, decreeing that the twenty-eight Regicides alone should go to execution, and that for the rest—the hatchet must be buried.

The bodies of Cromwell and Ireton were dug up and, having swung in clanking chains, the grim fruit of the gallows tree, were re-buried with public ignominy at Tyburn. Those who are interested will find the spot with ease. Face Hyde Park upon the south-western corner of Edgware Road, step off the pavement, and there inserted in the road about half-way between the kerb and the taxi-rank will be seen a triangular piece of steel. That is the spot where so many reprobates 'danced upon the empty air'.

Having satiated his loyal citizens with this senseless but harmless barbarity against the dead, Charles exerted himself to save the living. When he heard later of the excesses committed in his name by the new Royalist Governor, Sir William Berkeley, in far-away Virginia, he exclaimed angrily, 'That old fool has put to death more people in that naked country than I did here for the murder of my father.' At home, when only ten of the Regicides had paid the extreme penalty, the King scribbled some words upon a piece of paper and pushed it across the table to Clarendon. It read, 'I confess I am weary of hanging—let it rest.' And so, by his great clemency, even the majority of the Regicides were reprieved at last.

The third matter was even more difficult than the second, since it concerned 'Security of Tenure' for those who held lands formerly the property of the Crown, the Church, or the Cavaliers participant in the Civil War. Not unnaturally, everybody who had in any way served the Royalist cause expected their property back, and more if they could get it, but to have wiped out at one stroke every transaction in property which had taken place during the last eighteen years would obviously have been a terrible injustice to many. In a large number of cases lands originally confiscated or sold to assist the Royalist cause had changed hands a dozen times, the first purchasers were dead and the present owners men no less loyal than their original holders. What was to be done? Obviously there was no solution which could satisfy all parties, and so a middle course was taken—All lands which had been arbitrarily *confiscated* by the Commonweath were to returned to their first owners; lands *sold* by Royalists for whatever purpose were to remain the property of the present holders.

The Crown, the Church, and the Great Nobles came off well by this arrangement, while the country gentry fared badly. Hundreds of the latter had been compelled to sell their estates upon a falling market in order to pay the fines imposed by Parliament for having taken up arms on behalf of the King during the Civil War, or participation in Royalist risings at a later date. Now, at the Restoration, all their hopes of regaining their estates were dashed by a new law which debarred them from them for ever.

A howl of execration went up against the King, and on every side he was accused of base ingratitude towards those who had served him best. Yet he was only carrying out the promise to which his restoration had been subject, and it is difficult to see how else he could have dealt with this problem unless he was prepared to face another revolution.

This law giving 'Security of Tenure' becomes of first importance when considering Parliament's attitude to the King later in his reign. By it he unwillingly penalized the Cavalier Squires and alienated their affections. Their influence in Parliament, as we have already noted, was extremely strong, and it was very largely due to a desire to get their own back that they afterwards so consistently refused to vote him adequate funds.

The last and most difficult problem which he had to face as the result of the Declaration of Breda was his promise of 'Liberty of Conscience'.

There can be no doubt that Charles' personal views on the question of religion were a hundred and fifty years ahead of his time. He stood heart and soul for that attitude which has only become really general during the last fifty years—namely the belief 'That every man should have freedom to make his service to God in the manner which he considers best'—but to the great majority of the people of England at that time, such an attitude was regarded as almost worse than being an atheist.

It is difficult for us to realize today the intense and terrible bigotry which clouded the minds of otherwise sound and sensible men in the seventeenth century. The loathing which was engendered in our own population by an exceedingly able Ministry of Propaganda against the Germans in the first war gives but a vague idea of the attitude of the Nonconformists to the Anglicans, and of both against the Roman Catholics, in those days. Well-educated Englishmen were hypnotized in 1917 into believing that the Germans gouged out the eyes of our wounded, crucified their prisoners, and melted down their own dead in a corpse factory, that the human fat might be utilized for a variety of purposes. The people of France, Turkey, Montenegro and the Andaman Isles were all wrought up by the same type of nonsense into a fanatic blood lust against their own particular enemies. So, in the time of Charles II, Anabaptists really believed that Papists ate Protestant children and habitually committed sodomy with their wives. Quakers were so terribly convinced that the great mass of their countrymen were heading straight for very real and lasting flames that, as a method of protest, these otherwise sensible people stripped off their clothes and ran stark naked up and down the streets of the northern towns yelling, 'Woe! Woe! Woe to Yorkshire!' and all the other multitudinous sects up and down the land evinced the same wild unreasoning fear, hate, and dread of all who did not agree to their own particular form of ritual in the worship of a common God.

Patiently and tirelessly Charles grappled with this awful problem. From April to July of '61 he sat day after day in the Conference of Divines, endeavouring to wrest a little tolerance from first one party and then another, but the Cavaliers who had come into power at his Restoration were diehard Anglicans who had fought every bit as much for the complete supremacy of their Church as for the Crown.

To protect a minority of his people from an Anglican St. Bartholomew he was forced once more to take sides against the class who had served him best, and all their power in Parliament over the question of his finances was brought to bear against him.

Already that question of finance was giving the King considerable anxiety. The annual income of his father had been roughly £900,000, and his expenditure £1,100,000—and Charles found himself saddled with a debt of £530,000 contracted on that account before and during the Civil War. Expenditure under the Commonwealth had risen to the then appalling figure of £2,200,000 per annum. This enormous budget was the price which England had to pay for her increased prestige abroad under Cromwell's Government. Large fleets and standing armies must be paid for. During the early years of the

Commonwealth a considerable portion of the money had been raised by the sale of Crown lands and confiscated Cavalier estates, but such sources were by no means inexhaustible, and a year before the Restoration, England was groaning under a heavier taxation than had ever been known before—yet even this proved inadequate to balance the budget. On his return, therefore, the King found the annual deficit to be nearly £1,000,000, and an accumulated debt of over £2,000,000, in addition to the half-million owing to his father's account, and his own by no means small debts, contracted during fourteen years of exile. To meet these staggering commitments, the Exchequer showed upon examination the ludicrously inadequate sum of £11 2s. 10d.

Approached by the genial King upon the question of supplies, his faithful Commons proposed to make his revenue up to the sum of £1,200,000 per annum, and had Charles actually received this amount it would have proved quite adequate to his needs after the disbandment of the Army. The trouble was that he did not.

Cromwell's mailed fist may have scared Europe, but it had almost ruined the trade of the country. In consequence, the actual receipts from taxes voted by Parliament fell far below their estimated value. In the first year of his reign the unfortunate Charles only received £700,000 out of his paper £1,200,000, and during his first twelve years of Government the actual revenue averaged £400,000 per annum short of the necessary expenses.

By the summer of 1663, therefore, we find the King mildly reproving his Parliament with the words, 'There hath not appeared that warmth in you of late, in consideration of my revenue, as I expected,' but in the previous February he had, in conformity with his promise, declared for 'General Toleration', and the Anglican-minded Commons had grown very cold indeed.

It became obvious that if Charles was to secure sufficient supplies to carry on the affairs of the Kingdom, let alone pay off any portion of his enormous debts, he must give way to the Anglican frenzy which imbued the Parliament. In consequence he allowed four Acts dealing with the religious question to be passed.

The Corporation Act, by which no man could become a member of the municipal bodies which governed the towns and controlled the election of M.P.s unless he took an oath denying the lawfulness of taking up arms against the King, and—*received Communion according to the rites of the Church of England.*

The Act of Uniformity, by which every clergyman had to take a similar oath and assent to the New Anglican Prayer Book, which contained no less than 600 alterations, most of which were aimed at the Dissenters. To this Bill more than 2,000 of the Nonconformist clergy refused to submit, and in consequence a third measure was brought in.

The Five Mile Act, by which none of these two thousand were allowed to come with five miles of their former living in any town which possessed a Municipal Corporation, unless they took the oath under the Corporation Act. Upon this Charles did his best to secure pensions for the ejected ministers, and, seeing that they were all Nonconformists, his attitude in this matter should be borne in mind when considering those charges which have been brought against him by the Whig historians, who would have us believe that the only reason for his endeavours to secure 'Liberty of Conscience' was a personal leaning towards the Church of Rome. The Parliament rejected his humane amendment, and carried the Anglican campaign a stage further by a fourth measure.

The Conventicle Act; by it a conventicle was defined as a meeting of more than four persons outside any family for the purpose of religious celebration, and all such meetings other than those of the Church of England forbidden, under penalty of imprisonment for the first offence and transportation for the third.

Such, despite the King's hard-fought battle for Liberty of Conscience, were the laws decreed by the Cavalier Parliament in their determined attempt to crush out Dissenters and Catholics alike. But Charles did not surrender —he never surrendered anything. The tide might be running strongly against him for the moment and, like Canute, he realized the wisdom of stepping ashore, but no one knew better than he that everything comes to the man who knows how to wait. In the meantime, he set himself with quiet determination to blunt the weapons which were to be used for the persecution of these poor people on account of their religious beliefs. Parliament might make laws, and he be compelled to ratify them if the national services were to be saved from bankruptcy but in those days it was one thing to make laws and quite another to carry them out. Their execution depended very largely upon their energetic application by the officers of the Crown, and Charles succeeded in nullifying the effect of the persecution laws, to a very marked extent, by throwing large handfuls of grit into the machinery of justice.

In addition to the onerous business of endeavouring to straighten out the tangle in which the Commonwealth had left affairs at home, Charles was faced with the problem of Foreign Relations. Here he exercised the power of the prerogative to the full and refused to allow Parliament to interfere.

The Treaty of the Pyrenees had secured the peace of Europe just before the Restoration, and both France and Holland were bidding for the friendship of the English King. In Holland, after the death of Charles' brother-in-law, William II of Orange, ten years before, power had been seized by the popular party who approximated very nearly to the English Parliamentarians of the Civil War. France, on the other hand, was governed by a young and absolute Monarch, so that the natural sympathy of Charles gravitated towards the latter.

A far more important factor, however, lay in the commercial potentialities of the countries concerned. Spain and Portugal had passed out of their great century, and, exhausted by a long series of expensive wars, were slipping backwards in the race for the world's markets. France had never seriously counted in the commercial struggle, and so the battle lay between the English and the Dutch.

These were the two great maritime powers, and outside European waters the sailors of both nations waged an unceasing war for Commercial and Colonial supremacy. Charles, who throughout his whole reign sought to foster the trading ambitions of his subjects, saw clearly that every effort must be made to crush the Dutch.

In this his people were with him heart and soul, but unfortunately the question of religion came into the matter once more. Obviously the short road to victory over the Hollanders was alliance with the French, but the French were loathsome Papists, and although the English Protestant merchants were in a fine frenzy to take away the trade of the Dutch Protestant merchants, they fell into an agony of indecision between the equally urgent calls of their pockets and their consciences.

Pockets won, and in 1665 the English fleet set sail under James to drive the Dutchmen from the seas. He encountered them off Lowestoft and won a brilliant victory, twenty Dutch ships put out of action and their Admiral, Opdam, slain. That the action was not completely decisive was due to the cowardly deception practised by one unscrupulous man, Henry Brunker, a person of most unsavoury character, who had sailed with York as Groom of the Bedchamber. As night closed down on the battle, James went to rest, leaving orders that the Dutch should be closely pursued and himself awakened immediately his fleet was in touch with the enemy again. Sir William Penn, the Vice-Admiral, expressed an opinion that the second engagement would be even hotter than the first. When Brunker heard that, he gave orders purporting to be a message from the Duke that they should slacken sail immediately. When James awoke he found his fleet at a standstill and the Dutch disappearing far beyond the horizon.

A large number of young courtiers went with the fleet as volunteers. Rochester, who was interested in mystical speculation, made a pact with two others that if any of the three were killed they should reappear to the survivors. Both the others were killed beside him by a cannon ball, but neither reappeared, and their failure to do so caused him to remain sceptical regarding immortality for the rest of his life.

Buckhurst was also there and on the night before the action he composed the popular song which begins:

'To all you ladies now on land
We men at sea indite:
But first would have you understand
How hard it is to write—
The Muses now and Neptune too
We must implore, to write to you.'

Among those who lost their lives was young Lord Falmouth, a man very dear to the King so that he grieved bitterly when told his loss.

Even while England was rejoicing at the victory a terrible enemy was at work within her gates. The dread red crosses began to appear on the doors of the houses and soon the wealthier citizens of London were in full flight to the country, seeking safety from 'The Plague'. For four months previously there had been no rain, and the close-packed dens in the meaner part of the city quickly became charnel houses, loading the air with fresh disease. The remaining inhabitants were seized with terror and caught the contagion in the churches, where they clustered helplessly to pray or fell mortally stricken after wild orgies of debauch in the empty streets. All through that terrible winter and into the following spring the pestilence raged, and the melancholy cry 'Bring out your dead' could be heard in the silent streets each night.

Despite this affliction of the capital, the war went on. Charles removed his Parliament to Oxford and wrestled with it for supplies. He had equipped the Fleet entirely at his own expense, and now his credit had become so weak that even the City Bankers were refusing to lend him further money at so high a rate of interest as ten per cent. Yet somehow the King managed to carry on, and Pepys at the Navy Office did Herculean work in supervising the victualling of the Fleet. The Dutch coast towns were raided, and thirty-five enemy ships taken or sunk off the Wellbank.

Early in 1666, the French joined the Dutch under the obligation of an old Treaty, but England fought on undismayed. The Fleet through an error of judgment was now divided, Prince Rupert being set to watch the French in the Channel, and Albemarle the Dutch in the North Sea. On June the 1st, the latter gave battle to De Ruyter in spite of heavy odds; Rupert came to Albemarle's assistance on the second day, and for four succeeding days and nights a ghastly carnage ensued at sea. The Dutch were given a terrible gruelling, but after the battle the English Fleet returned almost shattered to its ports. However, within two months the surviving ships took their revenge and severely beat the Hollanders at the Weelings.

Buckingham was not among the gallants who volunteered for service, but remained at home engaged in a hectic love-affair with the Countess of Shrewsbury, a woman so notorious for her amours that it was said of her, 'as no person could boast of being the only one in her favour, so no man could complain of being ill-received'. Her husband alone seems to have remained unaware of her flagrant infidelities, but he learnt of her wild passion for the Duke, and challenged him immediately. The duel took place at Barns Elm on the 16th of January, and, as was the fashion of the times, each was accompanied by two seconds, who also fought. It was a desperate business, all six being seriously wounded. Shrewsbury was killed and one of Buckingham's seconds died later. It was said that during the encounter the lady, disguised as a page, held the Duke's horse, and that he slept with her that night 'all in his bloodie shirt', which gave great scandal to many.

Two months later he took her to live in his own mansion, and upon the Duchess protesting that it was impossible for herself and Lady Shrewsbury to live in the same house, he gave his wife the brutal reply, 'So I thought—and I have therefore ordered your coach to convey you to your father.'

In September another terrible blow fell upon England. The ubiquitous Pepys arrived hot and flustered one morning at Whitehall, bringing news that on the previous night a fire had broken out in Pudding Lane and, owing to an easterly gale, was spreading rapidly. Charles sent him with orders to the Lord Mayor that the houses in its path should be demolished, but by evening nothing had been done, and the King, who went out on to the river to view its lurid glare, realized the seriousness of the position. He realized, too, the hopeless incompetence of the Lord Mayor, and took command himself.

During the ensuing days and nights he fought the fire with courage and determination, blowing up houses, rewarding and encouraging his helpers, assisting in the demolitions, and passing buckets of water at the most dangerous points in person. On the fourth morning he stood ankle-deep in water, blackened and exhausted, with two-thirds of his capital lying in ruins about him, but his efforts had not been altogether in vain, for one of his subjects wrote of the matter: 'All that is left of the city and suburbs is acknowledged to be wholly due to the King and the Duke of York.'

The conflagration consumed 13,000 houses and 89 churches. 200,000 people were rendered homeless, but, amazing to relate, only eight lost their lives. The King busied himself immediately with alleviating the distress of the poor people who were camping in Moorfields, and in supervising plans for the rebuilding of the City. It was his wish to create a new and beautiful capital of broad streets and handsome squares as designed by his principal architect Sir Christopher Wren, but in this he was defeated by the obstinacy of the freeholders, who insisted on rebuilding on their old sites. Nevertheless, his regulations that the new houses should be of neat brick or stone, and of approved types, were strictly enforced. Large areas of slum dwellings had been swept away for ever, and Charles left London a far finer city than he found it.

Meanwhile the war dragged on. In February, '67, the Council realized that an immediate decision regarding the Fleet could no longer be delayed; reduced to an appalling plight by war, pestilence, and lack of supplies, it must either be completely re-equipped or laid up and paid off altogether. Charles' private credit was utterly exhausted, and Parliament stubbornly refused to vote monies for the maintenance of the services. The King, York, Rupert, Albemarle and the Archbishop protested at so drastic a measure, but they could produce no alternative suggestion, so Clarendon and the majority of the Council had their way, and the British Navy was allowed to remain unmanned and without equipment in its harbours.

The nerve of the nation had been shattered by the Plague and Fire. Commerce had been almost brought to a standstill, an anti-Papist scare was running through the country, and there was open insurrection in the North. In these straits, Charles decided that the only policy was a secret agreement for peace with France, and in this he employed 'Minette'. She had some years before married Philipe D'Orleans, brother of Louis XIV, and the French

Queen being a rather stupid invalid, Minette was now the most influential woman at the Court of France. To her assistance he sent the aged Jermyn, Earl of St. Albans since the Restoration, and by their united efforts a secret pact had been agreed with France by April.

While Louis was still busy negotiating a general pacification with the Dutch, their Fleet suddenly appeared in the Thames early in June, stormed Sheerness, sailed up the Medway, set fire to five English ships, and departed without let or hindrance, towing the *Royal Charles* captive behind them.

In vain Charles and his troops rode up and down the banks of the river, brandishing their swords and firing their pistols. Lacking a fleet, England had perforce to submit to this indignity.

Regarded soberly, the episode was by no means so terrible as it has been painted. Compare it, for example, with the brilliant exploit of Robin Holmes, who in the previous year had landed a thousand English on the Dutch coast at Schelling, sacked two towns, burnt *one hundred and fifty ships,* and destroyed a million pounds worth of Dutch property.

The trouble was, we had always been used to doing that sort of thing to other people and had never had it done to us. The raid itself had no more effect on the terms of the Treaty of Breda, which was concluded shortly afterwards, than the shelling of Scarborough and Whitby by the Germans in the first war had upon the Peace of Versailles.

By the Peace of Breda, the Dutch were compelled to secede the whole of their American Colonies, including the important city of New Amsterdam, which was re-christened, in honour of James, New York. The English thus became the undisputed masters of nearly 2,000 miles of the North American littoral, stretching in an unbroken line from the frozen pine forests of Northern Maine to the semi-tropical plantations of South Carolina.

The terms of the peace thus proved England victorious, yet to the mass of the people the Medway disaster was an unforgettable disgrace. It came as the crown to a long series of catastrophes, and general unrest had reached such a height that revolution was feared by many; it was even rumoured that the King, despairing of the situation, had fled abroad.

Charles, in this crisis, as usual, kept his head. He over-ruled his Council and called Parliament for July—immediately the tension slackened. Yet he was firm with them when they met, informing them politely that, 'Having given them one mark of his affection by summoning them in his need, he would now give them another by sending them home till October'. With this, and an assurance that it was not his intention to rule by force of arms, he dismissed them, but he knew that he must take drastic action in the intervening months if he wished to save his crown.

There was only one thing for it—Clarendon must go. He was old and ailing, tutorial in his manner to the King, and in recent years had proved himself incompetent, both in the management of Parliament and the war. He was hated by the Cavaliers, whom he had kept out of their estates; by the other members of the Council, who regarded him as a bar to progress; and by the people, for the ostentation of his vast new palace which he was building in Piccadilly. Charles' natural loyalty to an old friend and recognition of his former services had alone sustained him for so long. The King softened the blow to the best of his ability, and, after having listened patiently to the old man's abuse for two hours, left the room. As Clarendon passed down the steps of Whitehall for the last time, Castlemaine, dressed only in a smock, ran out of her aviary 'to bless herself at his going away', but something of Clarendon's past greatness returned to him at that moment in the dignity of his rebuke, 'Madame, you *too* will grow old.'

The dismissal of the Chancellor gave satisfaction to all parties, and the able Henry Bennet, Earl of Arlington, succeeded him as Charles' principal councillor.

Louis XIV had now taken the government of France into his own hands and was endeavouring to emulate Charlemagne. The whole of Europe stood watching, filled with the gravest perturbation as the Legions of 'Le Roi

Soleil', captained by the greatest generals of the age, swept in triumphant victory over vast tracts of territory. Arlington skilfully seized upon the situation to initiate a new foreign policy. He negotiated a treaty with the Dutch, into which Sweden was later drawn, thus forming the Protestant Triple Alliance to resist the aggrandizement of France and force peace upon Spain. These measures were greeted with the greatest delight, since the English, having satisfactorily crippled their commercial rivals, felt that they were now free to indulge their anti-Papist hatred, and Charles, as the leader of a Protestant Alliance, became for the moment the most popular of kings. He immediately took advantage of this temporary goodwill to place further impediments in the way of the execution of the Anglican Persecutionary laws.

In 1668, Parliament made a great to do about the accounts of the expenditure in the Dutch War. An inquiry was held and there was a general belief that out of the £4,000,000 which had all too late been voted for the Fleet, the King had put £1,000,000 in his own pocket. The unfortunate Pepys, who perhaps more than anybody was responsible for what little order there was in the chaotic affairs of the Navy, was called to the bar of the House to render an explanation of his accounts. He was not used to speech-making, and went to the ordeal in a terrible state of nerves, but his honest indignation at their cavilling leant him such eloquence that he spoke for two hours, giving chapter and verse as to the utilization of every penny, and thoroughly confounding his critics and the King's. His reward was a warm friendship of the King, which he retained to the end of the reign, and an admiration from his whole acquaintance which must have truly rejoiced his naïve, honest soul. To settle the matter once and for all, Charles added accountancy to his other duties and, having gone through all the papers personally, produced an audit proving beyond question that far from there having been any peculation, not only the whole of the sum voted by Parliament had been expended in a proper manner but a further million and a half, raised on his own rickety credit.

There now was born in the strictest secrecy the germ of the 'Grand Design', a new foreign policy which was to dominate the remainder of the reign. Minette, the only one of the family who had been brought up a Catholic, had a vision. She saw England and France united and the supreme rulers of the world, her brother-in-law, Louis, King of Europe, her dear Charles, King of the Seas and all the Lands beyond—and the latter brought safely back into the fold of Holy Mother Church. For two years she worked untiringly upon this project.

Charles at first conceded that he could see no objection to an understanding 'as between gentleman and gentleman', but pointed out that an open alliance would be impossible in the face of a hostile Parliament since he was dependent upon them for funds. This difficulty was overcome by the offer of liberal subsidies. He then stipulated that he should be asked nothing which might jeopardize the trade of Britain or her supremacy of the seas. The French gave in. Lastly, he was firm upon the point that he should not be required to violate his commitments under the Triple Alliance. Once more the French surrendered to his wish. From that time on the scheme gradually matured.

Whatever opinion one may hold of the morality of this pact, the negotiation of it shows Charles as the supreme diplomat of his time. By it he gained considerable sums of money which, while lightening the burden of the English taxpayer, would free him from the necessity of bargaining with Parliament for every subsidy he got, and enabled him to pursue that policy of Religious Toleration which was so near his heart. What the French gained it is difficult to see. Meanwhile, during the course of the negotiations, he was playing not with fire but dynamite. Had his intentions become known before the time was ripe, this Catholic alliance would undoubtedly have cost him his throne, and the vital necessity for extreme caution was the cause of the many delays before the project came to fruition. With an iron nerve he conducted this long and dangerous correspondence, and at the same time took his precautions against betrayal. In the latter, his personal character stood him in good stead, since the majority of those about him loved him with a devoted loyalty. Arlington, although a Protestant, was entirely to be trusted and was the first to be admitted to the dangerous secret; then York, already secretly converted to Rome; next the Catholics Arundell of Wardour and Thomas Clifford, a young, energetic and devoted minister. After these, Buckingham was involved, but only told a portion of the design. As protector of the Anabaptists, and therefore a power among the Puritans, he was used for cover, made to believe the idea was his own, and manoeuvred into pressing it through his hatred of Arlington, who pretended furious opposition—and all the while Charles was secretly consolidating his position. Commanders of doubtful loyalty were removed from forts and arsenals, to be replaced by trusted friends. The Army was freely exercised by him in person that he might win the attachment of his troops and officers, and the devoted Lauderdale coaxed through the Scottish Parliament an Act by which twenty-two thousand troops could be placed at the King's disposal for use in any part of his dominions.

Yet through all these months of skilful intrigue and manoeuvre, Charles remained to outward seeming the idle, dissipated Monarch. Lounging in his big chair, his women seated on cushions about him, he fondled the spaniels on his knees and bandied jests with Rochester. No sign was allowed to escape him of that terrible secret knowledge that if he were betrayed his whole Kingdom would flame into revolution.

In the summer of 1669, Louis revealed to him the secret overtures of De Witt for a Franco-Dutch partition of the Spanish Empire. Charles rightly felt that this relieved him of his obligations to Holland, and that he could now enter into a still closer alliance with France for a joint war to revenge the insult of the Medway.

At last Minette obtained leave from her jealous, impotent husband to travel to England. Seven days was all that His Meanness of Orleans would allow, although the brother and sister who loved each other so tenderly had not met for nine years—but it was enough. In a blaze of pageantry Charles received this frail, beautiful Princess, whose flame-like vitality was burning away her life, and every waking moment of those few brief days they spent together in an ecstasy of their spiritualized love. All too soon Henrietta sailed away with a last remembrance of her brother's dark, tear-dimmed eyes, but she carried with her his signature to the Treaty of her heart's desire. By the Treaty of Dover the King of England became the Pensioner of France, but he had not sacrificed the interests of Britain to his needs, and he was immeasurably strengthened in the future governance of his people for what he believed to be their truest interests.

SIX

The Snarling Pack

FOR the time being, Charles was master of the situation. With money in his pocket he could afford to indulge his policy of sending his Parliament for a holiday whenever they became too troublesome. In April, 1671, he prorogued them for nearly two years. Rochester's verse sums up the situation.

THE COMMONS PETITION TO THE KING

'In all Humility we crave,
Our Sovereign may be our Slave;
And humbly beg, that he may be
Betray'd by us most Loyally.
But if he please once to lay down
His Sceptre, Dignity and Crown,
We'll make him for the Time to come,
The greatest Prince in Christendom.'

THE KING'S ANSWER

'Charles, at this Time having no Need,
Thanks you as much as if he did.'

It was during these years, and the difficult ones which were to follow, that the King's leisure moments were brightened by the gay companionship of Pretty, Witty Nellie, 'The wildest creature that ever was at Court'.

Nell Gwynn's tender years were spent in the bawdy house of a Mrs. Ross, where she was wont 'to fill strong waters for the gentlemen'. Thence she took to selling oranges in the Pit at Drury Lane, and there Charles Hart, the actor—a great nephew of Shakespeare—found her, made her his mistress and put her upon the stage. The handsome Buckhurst saw her act and if we can believe Sir Carr Scrope, another of the wits:

'None ever had so strange an art
His passion to convey.
Into a list'ning virgin's heart
And steal her soul away.'

Buckhurst must have been a very attractive young man; in any case, it did not take him long to succeed with Nelly, and in July, 1667, he carried her off to Epsom, where, with Sir Charles Sedley, they 'kept merry house together' throughout a halcyon summer.

Epsom at that date was much what Bath became in the following century. In addition, it was near enough to London for the wealthier citizens to make a day's outing there on Sunday, and many a merry party took place at 'Clay Hill', 'Mawse's Garden', and 'The King's Head'.

It was at Epsom during that same summer that an incident causing great scandal occurred. Rochester, 'Gentle George'—as Etheridge was called—Captain Bridges and a Mr. Downes, having dined one night very much too well, proceeded to toss their hired fiddlers in a blanket. A barber came to the musicians' rescue, and then to save himself offered to take the four men to the lodgings of the sauciest and handsomest girl in Epsom; instead he took them to the Constable's house and there left them. To the officer's astonishment, the roisterers demanded immediate access to his wife, and on his refusing them they attacked his house, burst in his doors and broke his head. The poor man escaped and summoned the watch, upon which Etheridge made a drunken but submissive oration; thus pacified, they departed. Then Rochester treacherously drew his sword and lunged at the Constable. Downes, seizing him from behind, diverted the thrust, but on the Constable yelling 'Murder! ' the watch returned and, the others running off, the unlucky Downes first had his head cracked and then lost his life by being run through the side with a half-pike.

By the following January, Charles II had succeeded Charles Buckhurst as Nelly's lover, and with Charles Hart in mind, she used to refer to the King as 'my Charles the Third'. He settled her at a house in Pall Mall, but upon being presented with the lease, she tore it up and, although she was the least grasping of all Charles' mistresses, demanded a freehold. Charles smiled and gave it to her, and it is for that reason that there still remains today one gap in the Crown property which otherwise occupies the whole of the south side of Pall Mall. Nell did not finally leave the stage until some years later, although she bore a son to the King in May, 1670.

Her full-blooded vitality and rollicking wit were just the things which Charles needed to distract his mind from the eternal worries which pressed upon him, but he was incapable of remaining interested in one woman alone for long. When Minette came to Dover she had brought in her train the beautiful, baby-faced little Breton, Louise de Queroalle. Charles had been smitten at once and begged her of his sister, but poor Minette lay dead within a few weeks of her return to France, poisoned, it was said, but more probably stricken down by an attack of peritonitis. The King suffered an agony of sorrow, for she had held a place above all others in his affections, and the little Louise, whom he had so much admired, was sent from France to be a consolation.

He created her Duchess of Portsmouth, and in the conversation of this well-born little foreigner, Charles seemed to have derived a pleasure which none of his other mistresses could give. She retained a large share of his affections until his death, as also did the bawdy Nelly.

There was bitter rivalry between the two, of which Madame de Sévigné gives us an interesting picture. 'She (Louise) did not foresee that she should find a young actress in her way whom the King dotes on, and she has it not in her power to withdraw the King from her. He divides his care, his time, and his health between the two. The actress is as haughty as Mademoiselle. She insults her, she makes grimaces at her, she attacks her, she frequently steals the King from her and boasts whenever he gives her the preference. She is young, confident, wild, indiscreet, and of an agreeable humour. She sings, she dances, she acts her part with a good grace. She has a son by the King and hopes to have him acknowledged. As to Mademoiselle, she reasons thus: This Duchess pretends to be a person of quality, she says she is related to the best families in France, whenever any person of distinction dies she puts herself in mourning. If she is a person of quality, why does she demean herself to be a courtesan? As for me, it is my profession, and I do not pretend to be anything better.'

Nell won the hearts of the English people by her honesty, her gaiety and her generosity. Her father had died in Oxford Prison, and perhaps because of that her charities to prisoners were many, but the principal reason for her popularity was that she was English and Protestant. That she knew this herself is shown by her words when a hostile crowd mobbed her sedan at Oxford in mistake for that of the hated 'Mrs. Carwell'. Poking her curly head out of the window, she cried, 'Pray, good people, be civil—I am the *Protestant* Whore.' Upon which she was borne on her way midst ringing laughter and a chorus of bawdy good wishes.

She did not forget her old mother in her rise to prosperity, and kept that good lady well supplied with gin, so well in fact that, staggering home one night, old Mrs. Gwynn fell in a ditch by Westminster and was drowned. On this occasion Etheridge belied his sobriquet of 'Gentle George' and composed this by no means kind epitaph:

'The Pious Mother of this Flaming Whore.
Maid, Punk and Bawd full sixty years or more,
D'yd drunk with Brandy on a Common Shore.'

In 1775 another Duchess came to adorn the cushions about Charles' easy chair—the lovely Hortense Mancini, Duchesse de Mazarin, whom the too cunning Cardinal had denied him as a bride only six months before his triumphant Restoration. It has been said that the life of Hortense 'might well adorn a tale'. Cultured, amorous, bewitchingly beautiful, the heroine of a hundred strange adventures, she sought refuge at the Court of Charles from the persecution of her husband, a religious maniac, who kept her up all night to pray. She occupied a charming house at Chelsea and lives immortal in the letters of another exile, the great epicurean philosopher St. Evremond, who was her neighbour, platonic lover, and constant companion till her death.

Assessing Charles' women as a whole, it is doubtful if any prince in modern, as opposed to ancient, times ever gathered together a finer seraglio. In numbers, compared to certain other sovereigns, they were not excessive; but Charles was a connoisseur, and each of the six great mistresses possessed some outstanding quality of wit, intellect, or passionate loveliness which made her a real personality. Even Frances Stewart, stupid as she may have been in other ways, had, in addition to her beauty, the by no means inconsiderable distinction of being the best-dressed woman at his elegant and splendid Court.

It is, perhaps, partly this factor which has resulted in more prominence being given to his amours than those of equally dissolute but less fastidious kings. Yet the man who demands personality in addition to beauty in his loves must pay the price, unless he is prepared to be faithful to his choice, Charles, incapable as he was of remaining devoted to any one woman over a period of years, suffered considerably from the jealousy and intrigue of the others whenever he brought a new inmate to the Royal bed.

He could, of course, like other monarchs, have dismissed them when he wearied of their favours, or kept them in subjection by the threat of some practical manifestation of the Royal displeasure. If he had followed that course he would have spared himself many petty worries, but such an attitude was foreign to his nature. They were all old friends with whom he had spent many happy hours, and therefore, even at the expense of much trouble to himself, there could never be any question of disgrace or punishment. Instead they must be allowed their freedom to live at Court upon the handsome pensions which he made them.

Unfortunately, by some strange freak of nature, the majority of women respond more readily to rougher treatment by their men. nor for some reason are they often faithful to the lover possessed of the human understanding which prompts him to condone their follies and forgive their faults.

Charles' lack of a capacity to hurt his women debarred him from gaining the entire devotion of any one of them except Nell—although it is doubtful if even she considered him a *great lover*—and, curiously enough, his Queen.

To the rest he was an extremely competent amorist, the most amusing of companions, and a man whose fathomless generosity made him easy game. They were a greedy, rapacious lot, and lost no opportunity of plaguing and tormenting him for gifts and honours while they conducted flagrant infidelities with other men.

The cynical King can never have been their dupe, but he preferred to bear with them as lovely, wicked children, rather than have to reproach himself for ingratitude—not for the services which they had rendered but for the relaxation and pleasure which they had enabled him to take to himself in their company when harassed by those weighty problems which constantly beset him.

After the mourning for Minette, the merry suppers and galas at the Theatre went on once more. Buckingham turned playwright and produced his *Rehearsal*, a rollicking farce in which the heavy mannerisms of the other dramatists were deliciously satirized. Admittedly he was aided in its composition, but he was the principal author of the piece and undoubtedly possessed a high critical faculty.

In one of Dryden's plays the heroine, in as moving and affected a tone as she could muster, had to speak the line:

> 'My wound is great—because it is sc small,'

and having spoken, paused, looking the very picture of woebegone beauty. Upon which Buckingham immediately sprang up in his box, and cried in a ringing voice:

'Then t'would be greater—were it none at all.'

The house dissolved in tears of mirth, and the incident cost poor Dryden his benefit night.

The mad Duke had no more respect for the pulpit than the stage, as witness a scene in the Chapel Royal. A young and bashful preacher had been chosen to deliver his first sermon. In accordance with the custom of the day he wore black gloves, and, the dye chancing to be of inferior quality, when he drew his hand across his perspiring face, long black streaks appeared, which gave him the most ludicrous appearance. He then announced his text: 'Behold! I am fearfully and wonderfully made.' Buckingham did not attempt to restrain his amusement, but gave one gigantic guffaw of laughter which had the effcct of discharging the pent-up mirth of the whole Court upon the unfortunate divine.

Charles was the ever-present centre about which this gay world revolved. He was one of those clever people who, while actually very busy, always seem to have abundance of time. He hunted the stag at Windsor, indulged his passion for the 'Sport of Kings' at Newmarket, amused himself by pitting the wit of his mistresses against one another in Whitehall. Yet in the solitude of the little cabinet behind his bedchamber—to which William Chiffinch alone in all the land had entry, and where he kept his treasured collection of antiques and clocks—he worked steadily upon his secret policy.

All the ministers of the CABAL, Clifford, Arlington, Buckingham, Lauderdale, and even Ashley Cooper, the rabid Protestant Earl of Shaftesbury, had now been involved, although the latter was not permitted to know the terms of the innermost treaty of all, whereby Charles had promised to accept Conversion and declare himself a Catholic.

In this last matter the King showed no eagerness, and he must have derived considerable amusement from composing letters excusing his delay to the earnest-minded Louis. At first 'the Pope was dying, and he would not undertake so great a step with the Holy Father in that condition'. Then he really felt 'that an Englishman should be given the honour of his conversion and he had no one suitable about him', and, lastly, 'the divine concerned must also be a chemist, that he might be capable of resolving certain scientific doubts which still lingered in his mind'—and, of course, Charles knew quite well that, learned as the prelates of the Roman Church might be, there was not one among them quite so erudite as that.

The last excuse was by no means so thin as it may sound, for all the world knew that he was deeply interested in science and spent many hours in his laboratory. This interest formed one of the principal links in his friendship with the otherwise irresponsible Buckingham, who spent much time and an incredible amount of money in his search for the Philosopher's Stone.

Another deeply interested in scientific research was that queer, macabre figure the King's uncle, Prince Rupert of the Rhine. From the dashing cavalry leader of the Civil Wars he had passed to years of strange adventure with the remnant of the Royalist Fleet as a buccaneer upon the Spanish Main, then after the Restoration he had held high command in the naval war against the Dutch. After the war his restless spirit had sent him out in '68 as leader of the English Russian Company's expedition to the North, and in '70 Charles had presented him with the Charter for the establishment of the Hudson's Bay Company. Now, having explored the waters of both hemispheres, this rough, passionate man set himself to unravel the secrets of the laboratory, and amongst other things we owe to him the discovery of the art of mezzotinto.

The King's experiments were of a more practical nature than those of the other two. He founded the 'Royal Society' and was a constant attendant at their meetings. In his humorous vein he could not resist twitting them with 'spending all their time *weighing air*', and once perplexed their proceedings for a whole month by demanding a solution of the problem: 'Why is it that a bucket of water into which a fish has been thrown weighs no more after the fish has been put in than it did before?' How he laughed, too, when it was reported, with great excitement, that Sir Paul Neal had discovered an elephant in the moon—and on investigation it turned out to be only a mouse that had got into the wrong end of the telescope. But Charles also possessed a very sober side, and it is not too much to say that by his personal encouragement, patronage, and protection of enquiring minds such as Sir Isaac Newton's, the seeds were sown for the great harvest of scientific knowledge reaped in the following century.

In March, 1672, all the principal men in the Council now being a party to the Treaty with the French, Charles felt himself strong enough to issue an Indulgence suspending the penal laws against Roman Catholics and Dissenters alike. The anti-Papist feeling in the country had been growing by leaps and bounds, so the measure brought forth a storm of abuse; but the attention of the nation was largely distracted by his honouring his other obligations under the Treaty, and declaring war upon the Dutch.

At the same time, Louis' enormous armies advanced to the attack through Flanders, and it seemed for the moment as if the Dutch would be completely overwhelmed. Yet the courage of this little nation, which had resisted the might of Spain in the previous century, proved equal to the ordeal. They revolted against their Parliamentary Party, murdered its leader, De Witt, and placed power in the hands of Charles' young nephew, William III of Orange. De Ruyter, with his Fleet, came upon James, watering in Southwold Bay, and at once gave battle. The action was fought in a ghostly fog, amidst blinding smoke, with the ships locked at close quarters. Both navies suffered terrible casualties, but the Dutch escaped destruction and for the remainder of the war gave England as good as they got. On land, the energetic young sovereign, afterwards to be William III of England, employed a mightier power than Louis' hundred and twenty thousand troopers. By opening his dykes he devastated great areas and caused terrible distress, but the roaring waters annihilated the French advance, and by this drastic measure he saved his country.

Early in 1673 Charles found himself in financial straits again. The war had cost him more money than he had received in subsidies from France; thus he was in an even worse position than he had been before the signing of the Treaty of Dover. There was nothing for it but to summon Parliament. They met in an angry, threatening mood, determined not to vote one penny unless Charles abandoned his policy of Toleration. With vigorous firmness the King resisted their demands, and for the moment it looked like Civil War. Then Louis intervened, begging Charles rather to surrender on the question of religion than divide the country so that it could no longer assist him against the Dutch. Reluctantly, Charles withdrew his Declaration of the previous year, but worse was to come.

The Parliamentary bigots made the grant of funds for the continuation of the war subject to the passing of the Test Act. By this, all persons refusing to take the Anglican Sacrament and an oath against the Catholic doctrine of Transubstantiation were declared incapable of holding public office.

This measure broke the CABAL. Young Clifford, one of Charles' staunchest friends, had to surrender his staff of office; Arlington, suddenly filled with unexpected weakness and vacillation, retired. Buckingham openly went over to the enemy, and Shaftesbury intrigued against his master, secretly plotting the divorce of the poor, barren, Catholic Queen.

It was a desperate spring and summer. Fuel was added to the anti-Catholic fire by the open knowledge that James, the heir to the throne, was a declared Romanist. He was forced to resign his post as Lord High Admiral, and, Anne Hyde being dead, Parliament was filled with added fury at the choice of his new bride, the young Catholic Princess Mary of Modena. Rupert, with ill-equipped and insufficient ships, was hard put to it to prevent a repetition of the Medway. The treasury was empty, revolution in the air, and the Council at loggerheads, not one of them having a policy to offer which might bring the nation back to sanity.

Charles alone kept his head, replying merrily enough to an anxious enquirer, 'The truth is that this year the

Government (meaning himself, of course) thrives marvellously well, for it eats, and drinks, and sleeps as heartily as I have ever known it; nor does it vex and disquiet itself with that foolish, idle, and impertinent thing called business.' But, although he put a bold face on it for the benefit of his enemies and the idle crowd, in secret he was worried and anxious.

With the long, lazy stride that other people found it so difficult to keep up with, he walked miles of country that summer, dark-faced and thoughtful, missing nothing of the ever-growing panic around him, yet disclosing his secret mind to no man. Then in October, when Parliament met again—filled with the same angry spirit of revolt which its predecessor had shown against his father in '41—he acted. After a nine days' session, to save the faithful Lauderdale from impeachment, he closed the House till January, dismissed the treacherous Shaftesbury, and to the amazement of the nation placed power in the hands of Thomas Osborne, Earl of Danby.

The King never liked Danby, but his decision was nothing less than a stroke of genius. It was the first time that it had occurred to any Monarch to rule a fractious Parliament through their own chosen leader. Danby was an Anglican, a Cavalier and, more important still, a first-class business man. He alone was able to persuade his followers that, unless the country was to go to rack and ruin, they *must* grant adequate funds to carry on the necessary services of state.

In the meantime, Charles dealt equally skilfully with foreign affairs. He put it to Louis that the war was costing more than the amount received from France, which had not been the intention of the pact, therefore Louis must balance accounts or the war was off. Louis refused an adequate amount, so Charles opened negotiations with the Dutch. They, too, were utterly exhausted, and happy to buy a peace by which they agreed to secede the right of dipping to the English flag, and to pay an indemnity of £200,000. Thus, despite all the difficulties with which he had been beset, Charles brought the war to a victorious conclusion, and from that time on Britain became the undisputed Mistress of the Seas.

The power of the Dutch having been broken, the benefits of trade began to accrue to England, and in the following year the beginnings of a new prosperity were felt throughout the land. By this, Danby's task was greatly facilitated, and in the following year the receipts from Customs and Excise rose to such a degree that for the first time in the reign income at last balanced expenditure. In this period of good fortune it stands to Charles' honour that he did not forget his old creditors. Two years' compound interest was allotted to the bankers who had suffered so severely by the closing of the Exchequer, and the King even managed to pay off the last instalments of his father's debts with which he had been struggling all these years.

Happy times might have ensued and the people come to a better understanding of their Prince but for the embittered vanity and ambition of one unscrupulous man. Shaftesbury, the disgraced ex-Minister, set himself, with a zeal worthy of a better cause, to stir up strife and bring discredit on the Monarchy. He took up his residence in the City and initiated a tireless campaign against the Court, supervising the issue of a thousand scurrilous pamphlets and fanning the flames of rebellion by impassioned speeches to the malcontents who gathered at the Green Ribbon Club.

Shaftesbury's efforts resulted in the formation of the Whig Party, pledged to overthrow the Tories under Danby and to exterminate the Catholics by an English Protestant Inquisition. The type of man who made up the better elements of his following may be judged by the seventeen Gloucestershire Lords who sent a remonstrance to the King. 'Among them there was not one who either to himself or to his father could lay claim to any honourable service performed either to the King or *his* father during the time of the great rebellion.' As to the worst elements, they were the fanatics and madmen who pester every Government—the human dock rats from Wapping, the hooligans, the jail-birds, and the very scum of the London gutters.

Buckingham also took up his residence in the city and hobnobbed with the old republicans to the vast amusement of Charles, who dubbed him 'Alderman George'; whilst Rochester, the perpetual jester, banished from the Court for another libellous satire on the King, enlivened these dark days by setting up on Tower Hill disguised as an astrologer. The great world flocked to see him, and came away marvelling at Doctor Alexander Bendo's uncanny knowledge of their pasts. He also carried on a roaring trade in quack medicines, giving particular attention to dubious draughts guaranteed to kill—or relieve young women of unwanted progeny.

Danby, with his Anglican sympathies, was strongly in favour of a policy to resist the aggrandizement of France, and, despite Charles' assurance that he would never permit a war against his old ally, Louis became extremely frightened. He therefore adopted new tactics and took as his love the strangest of all bedfellows for an abs[illegible]te and Catholic King—the English Whig Party. Ba[illegible]on, the French Ambassador, was duly instructed, and during the next few years many thousands of pounds passed through his hands into the ready palms of the Whig Lords, that these patriots might firmly resist the passing of any vote of supplies through the House which should enable England to go to war.

For five years the struggle between Danby's pro-Dutch Anglicans and Shaftesbury's pro-French Nonconformists was waged with ever-increasing bitterness. In '77 the Minister gained a brilliant victory by negotiating the marriage of Mary—James' eldest daughter and grand-daughter to old Chancellor Clarendon—with William of Orange. He thus provided for a Protestant succession, and so popular was the alliance with the mass of the people that for the moment it looked as if Shaftesbury and his Whigs were completely undone. Yet in the autumn of the following year a terrible scourge was to be brought into play upon the party that upheld the Crown.

Titus Oates, a grim and sinister figure, made his appearance and laid an information before Sir Edmund Berry Godfrey, a London magistrate, regarding a 'Popish Plot'. All was in readiness, so ran his tale, to kill the King, set the Romanist James upon the throne, land a French Army and force Catholicism upon England by the sword. The prompt acceptance of this amazing story was greatly facilitated by the disappearance of the magistrate to whom it had been told, and the discovery of his dead body in a ditch near Primrose Hill some days later. It was immediately assumed that he had been murdered by the Papists.

Shaftesbury seized with avidity upon the incident and stirred the anti-Catholic mob into a frenzy of fear and panic. Oates was deemed the saviour of his country, voted a pension, and brought before the King.

From the very beginning, Charles, with his shrewd

common sense, had been sceptical about the man. The fact that Oates had been expelled from his school, the Navy, and two Jesuit colleges—and in addition had been twice convicted of perjury—did not beget confidence in any sane examiner, and now his strange appearance was far from that of an open, honest man. His head was like a vast, inverted U, he had no neck, a horrid fleshy face, with a straight gap for mouth, and little cunning eyes, but his lies concerning this gigantic conspiracy, in which every Catholic of any importance in the whole of Europe seemed to be involved, were fashioned with considerable adroitness.

Charles examined him in person and twice caught him out in an obvious lie. First, by asking what Don John, who was supposed to be in the conspiracy, looked like—to which Oates, knowing the majority of Spaniards to be dark, replied, 'A tall, black-haired man', when actually he was short and fair—the second time by enquiring the whereabouts in Paris of the Jesuit College. Oates said, 'Neare the Louvre,' upon which Charles shrugged with disgust, 'As well say Gresham College stands in Westminster.'

Unfortunately the King's subjects were by no means as level-headed as himself. With amazing rapidity the wildest rumours gained complete credence. The good people of London expected any night to be murdered in their beds, and took to carrying arms whenever they went abroad. The invasion scare heightened the terror of the population, and, although we may regard it now as childish panic, it should be remembered that there were people living then whose fathers had helped to resist the Spanish Armada, which was a very real threat of invasion indeed.

Fuel was added to the fire by the discovery and publication of Coleman's correspondence with the Jesuit Confesssor of Louis XIV. Actually his letters were nothing but the irresponsible outpourings of an indiscreet fanatic, but, since he held the position of secretary to the Duchess of York, they gave a terrible semblance of truth to the wild inventions of Oates' fertile brain, and the whole country was wrought to a fever pitch of fear and anger.

The only episode in modern history which can give some idea of the fanatical excitement caused by the anti-Catholic agitation is the anti-Jewish mania which sent the whole French nation mad during the years of the Dreyfus case. Sound, moderate men no longer dared to utter a word of doubt regarding the wildest statements of Oates and his brother informers; to do so was to lay themselves open to an immediate charge of being Papists themselves. People began to distrust even their oldest friends, and soon a reign of terror held the country in its grip. Even the honest Pepys was arraigned through the machinations of his personal enemies, accused of being a Papist and, on the flimsy evidence of having purchased an old painting of the Crucifixion from an antique dealer some years before, flung into the Tower.

Coleman and a number of Jesuit Priests were tried for Sir Edmund's murder, and although the King examined them in person before his Council and tore their evidence to shreds, it made no difference to the madness of the nation, or the verdict of the Courts, which straightway condemned them. Charles protested at this manifest injustice, but Shaftesbury's mob howled for their execution. To have interfered with the decision of the English Courts of Justice would have given Shaftesbury the very excuse he wanted to start a civil war, so for the sake of the nation Charles had to let the law take its course, saying, as he appended his signature to the warrants, 'Let the blood lie on those that condemn them, for God knows I sign with tears in my eyes.'

Oates, now the idol of the mob and Parliament alike, even had the temerity to accuse the Queen of complicity in a plot to poison her husband. Catherine was distraught with grief at this dastardly attack, but she had a true protector in the King. With sudden fury he rounded on his tormentors, threw Oates into prison and cried angrily, 'They think that I have a mind to a new wife, but for all that I will not see an innocent woman abused.'

Montagu, the ex-ambassador to France, now turned traitor and made public Danby's correspondence. The

Secret Treaty of Dover, by which the King had promised to become a Catholic, and all the subsequent negotiation, came to light. Shaftesbury made tremendous capital out of these disclosures, people began to believe that Charles himself was in the Catholic plot, and the Whigs proceeded to the immediate impeachment of the Minister Danby.

It was in these dark days that Charles said to his old intimate Sir John Reresby, 'Fear not. I will stick by you and my old friends, for if I do not, I shall have nobody to stick by me.' Danby he had never liked, but he had proved a loyal servant and so, true to his word, the King stood by him in his need. Parliament, although embittered, was still the old Cavalier Parliament which had been elected eighteen years before, and in it there still lingered at bottom some elements of its first fine loyalty. A general election at such a time of unrest and hostility meant for a certainty that the old King-haters would top the polls. After that, with Shaftesbury urging them on to revolution, all was darkness. Yet, to save his minister, Charles determined to face whatever fate might bring, and took the most perilous step in all his reign by dissolving Parliament.

His fears were only too soon realized—when the new Parliament met in 1679 the Republicans were in an overwhelming majority. Immediately they opened the battle on the question of the Succession, which had been smouldering for some time. York was a hated Papist, so they demanded that, if he succeeded, his children should be taken from him and his power hedged about with every possible restriction, or, better, that James should be excluded altogether and Monmouth, the King's eldest son, a Protestant, legitimized.

Charles made an effort to convert his brother, but, as usual, James proved stubborn, so it was thought best that he should leave the country for a time while the King continued to grapple with the anti-Catholic madness.

Monmouth was a fine figure of a man—handsome, graceful, affable—the idol of his father and the populace alike. With diabolical skill, Shaftesbury had set the son against the father, filling the young man's head with wild ambitions, but Charles would not suffer him to oust his uncle from his rights. That summer Monmouth had been sent against the rebellious Scots and defeated them at the battle of Bothwell Bridge, but his semi-royal progress through the country had annoyed the King, who knew that for all his beauty he was an empty-headed lad ignorant of the dangerous game that he was being made to play for the furtherance of Whig intrigue. In consequence, Charles deprived him of his Generalship and publicly declared his illegitimacy, exploding once for all the story that his own marriage contract with Lucy Walter lay hidden in some mysterious black box.

Parliament was furious, for they had taken Monmouth

to their hearts, and retaliated by criticizing Charles for the expenditure necessary to the upkeep of his other illegitimate children, of which he now had quite a number.

By Castlemaine there had been Charles, Henry, and George Fitzroy—now made Dukes of Southampton, Grafton and Northumberland—besides three daughters. As Duchess of Cleveland, their mother remained at Court, an expensive pensioner, but Charles had long since ceased to visit her. The break had come when he had arrived one day unexpectedly at her apartments and a young man had been forced to jump out of the window. It was John Churchill, then a cornet in the guards but later to become the famous Duke of Marlborough.

Portsmouth had borne him Charles Lennox, Duke of Richmond; Moll Davies a daughter, Mary Tudor; Catherine Peg, Charles FitzCharles, Earl of Plymouth; and Lady Shannon another daughter, Charlotte, Countess of Yarmouth.

There still remained Nell Gwynn who had done her duty by presenting him with two sons, and on one occasion when he was at her house she called them to her, 'Come here you little bastards.' 'Nell! Nell!' the King protested, 'can'st thou not modify thy language?' to which she gave the promptly reply, 'Well! and what other names have I to call them by?' Charles took the hint and created the eldest Duke of St. Albans.

In criticizing his expenditure upon his children, the

Commons forgot that he lacked a legitimate family, which might have cost them more without their having any pretext for complaint. Actually, his progeny cost the nation very little, for when they reached their teens he married them off, one after the other, to the richest heiresses in England.

The year 1679 aged the King considerably. Only his marvellous power of foreseeing every move made in the game by his enemies enabled him to avert civil war—and that he was determined to prevent at any cost. Throughout the Catholic persecution the so-called 'Merry Monarch' stood alone and friendless, middle-aged now, and saturnine—troubled and anxious yet never in the most trying circumstances giving way to those fits of irritable temper to which crowned heads have shown themselves so prone when affairs of state go contrary to their will. The mongrel pack might snap and snarl about his knees, but he was the master still and they could not pull him down.

Shaftesbury, with devilish cunning, now set himself to subvert the justice of the land. The Sheriffs of London were responsible for the selection of all juries, and the Earl secured the election of two of his most trusted adherents as the Sheriffs—henceforth the decisions of the Courts became a mockery. However upright the judge might be, he was compelled to accept the verdict of these juries, packed exclusively with Shaftesbury's fanatic followers. Charles could do nothing unless he broke from his principle 'To govern by the known laws of the land'. Bitterly he ratified the unjust decisions of the Courts, rather than give his enemies a legitimate excuse for rebellion, yet he adhered to his formula with dogged courage and would not suffer them to infringe the constitution by one particle.

To quiet the country he agreed to govern without a Cabinet and reduce his Privy Council; then once again he employed his old policy of 'kicking people upstairs'. Shaftesbury and his crew were admitted to the Council. One loyalist protested at the exclusion of his father in this reshuffle, and, taking him by the arm, Charles patiently explained, 'Doth he imagine that I left him out because I did not love him? He was left out because I do love him. But keep this to thyself.'

In July, to Shaftesbury's fury, the King dissolved his second Parliament, and a little gleam of light showed in the darkness of the persecution. Chief Justice Scroggs, not to be bribed or brow-beaten—and in the face of terrible hostility—acquitted Wakeman, the Queen's physician, then rounded on the informers for the perjurers they were, which set sounder men athinking. Yet the new Parliament which met in August pressed more strongly than ever for James' exclusion, and the 'Popish Terror' showed little sign of any real abatement.

In October the King dismissed Shaftesbury from his

Council, and the embittered Earl took up his quarters in the City once more, busying himself with another Popish scare, 'The Meal Tub Plot', which brought about a renewed frenzy of anti-Catholic feeling.

All through 1680 the grim struggle went on, Shaftesbury beating up his paid informers to bring yet more false accusations, and deluging the country with libellous pamphlets against the King; while his lieutenants stirred up trouble in Ireland, disclosing another fake conspiracy there with the object of discrediting the loyal Ormonde and forcing him to resign. But here at least he met his match. The great Duke was not the man to be intimidated by such scum, and wrote to his master, 'It maketh me only the more resolved to serve thee, with all the vigour that time hath left me, and all the loyalty that no time can take away.'

That magnificent testimony remains for Charles against all the libels of the Whig historians. Ormonde stands above reproach. Anglican, upright, courageous, sane, one of the finest figures in English history. When he wrote it he had known the King intimately as boy and man for fifty years, and unprincipled, despotic kings do not beget such splendid loyalty in their greatest servants.

Charles, through the Whig opposition, was now almost reduced to beggary. In December, Parliament passed a resolution that whosoever should advance him money was a national enemy, and Shaftesbury prepared a measure for securing to his party all the strong places in the land. Once more the country was on the verge of civil war.

In the New Year the only course was for the King to dissolve this, his *third*, Parliament, and that the next might at least be freed from intimidation by Shaftesbury's 'brisk boys' and the hooligan mob, Charles summoned it to Oxford.

On March 21st, 1681, the *fourth* Parliament of the reign assembled, no less truculent than the last, with armed retainers, and 'No Popery' badges in their hats. Once more they fiercely demanded James' exclusion, but they had quarrelled with France, so with speed and secrecy Charles acted. Playing upon Louis' renewed fears of war, he juggled him into renewing his own subsidies as the price of peace.

On March 27th the Exclusion Bill was laid upon the table. In his ordinary clothes Charles walked to the Chamber. 'Better one master than five hundred,' he remarked thoughtfully to a young member in the robing-room, then he entered the Assembly. He had prorogued one Parliament to save Lauderdale, dissolved another to save Danby, now he was about to finish with Parliament for good to save his brother.

With a dark, stern face he addressed these would-be Kommissars from the throne. 'I will never use arbitrary government myself, and I am resolved not to suffer it in others.'

Thus, after a session of only six days, he dismissed them. It was the one step which in the state of the country they had thought he would not dare to take—but they lacked the courage to defy him. Angry, silent, bewildered, they slunk away—never again to be allowed to meet during his kingship.

SEVEN

The Verdict of the People

FOR twenty years Charles had prorogued and dissolved his Parliaments at every serious crisis. Now he had done with them for good, and henceforth he was to reign alone. It is this period which enables the historians of the last century to hurl the epithet 'Despot' at him with so much gusto.

From the beginning of his reign, Parliament had consistently refused to grant Charles adequate funds to maintain the services of State unless he was prepared to sanction laws which he knew would entail great hardship to a large section of the community.

His attitude has been paralleled by that of our greatest statesman in later times for the governance of the coloured people of the Empire. He and they equally maintained that religious minorities must be protected from the hatred and persecution of fanatical majorities holding a different faith. Unfortunately his Parliaments were incapable of appreciating this high conception, so he elected to ignore them and keep the services going as well as he was able on subsidies from France.

Once again it should be borne in mind that England gave nothing in return for these subsidies. Louis only paid for protection from a war which Charles in any case had no intention of waging.

It has been said that our prestige abroad suffered during his reign, but those who say it can have little knowledge of the facts. Much capital has been made out of his sale of Dunkirk shortly after the Restoration. If his income had been the £2,200,000 which Cromwell drew from a groaning land there would have been no necessity. As it was, his revenue at that time was only a little over £700,000, and Dunkirk cost £130,000 a year to keep up; moreover, it could only have proved a focus for continual trouble, and in the circumstances its sale was a wise piece at statesmanship. Another reason urged was his abandonment, late in the reign, of Tangier. It had been his hope to make it into a base for British trading in the Mediterranean, and he spent over £2,000,000 on it. Unfortunately little was known at home of the geography and conditions in this then far distant port, and only when proper surveys had been carried out was it realized to be impossible of defence. Hills ringed the town and from them hostile tribesmen dominated the defences of the garrison. Wisely, therefore, Charles decided to squander no more treasure upon its upkeep, and sent Dartmouth with the faithful Pepys to demolish the fortifications and evacuate the town.

Contrast these two minor episodes in a reign lasting for nearly a quarter of a century, with the power and prestige of Britain advancing by leaps and bounds across the Seven Seas to millions of acres of rich territory. Bombay established as the Gate to India, the coast of Guinea opened up and already shipping home the gold and ivory out of Africa. The whole of the North American seaboard from Maine to Carolina in our possession, and thence, by 2,000 miles of islands, our power stretching to the northern coast-line of the southern continent. The Mediterranean made free to English ships by skilful treaties with the Turk and Moor. The Hudson's Bay Company already at work which was to gain Canada for the Crown, while nearer home the most powerful King in Europe, Louis of France, was paying us a yearly subsidy rather than face us in a war, and the Dutch, our only serious rivals, lay humbled and broken, so that our merchant navy became the carriers of the world, and Britain —from Charles' time onward—the undisputed Mistress of the Seas.

All these endeavours which later were to bear such wondrous fruit were, unlike the early ventures such as the *Mayflower* in the previous reign, things near the King's own heart. He loved the sea himself aud every seaman knew him for a friend, ever ready to pore with them over maps and charts, and plan new expeditions into distant seas. It was his reward that he should live to see the first-fruits of his labours, and it was largely these which saved him from the fury of the rebellious Whigs.

In the middle of the battle with Shaftesbury, Charles fell ill, and so seriously that for a few days his life was despaired off. An amazing revulsion of feeling swept through the country—What if he should die? For years the Whigs had been trying to force a civil war upon him, and suddenly all moderate men realized whither they were being driven by the politicians. King-baiting had become a game, for, badger him as they would, Charles always managed somehow to keep the peace—but if he died? James, the Catholic bigot, would succeed. Protestant Monmouth would go out against him, and civil war would become an actual fact. With sudden horror they recalled the terrible years when the country had been rent with strife; the executions, the fines, the savage tyranny of Ireton, Lambert, Harrison, the gruelling taxation of the Lord Protector. They looked at their fields of smiling corn and saw them seized for the Army that they hated, looked at their bank balances growing year by year, while Europe fought and England lived at peace—and saw them taken; looked to every port in Britain filled with the argosies that brought home the riches of the world—and saw them sunken, captured, commandeered. In sudden terror they crowded to the churches to pray that Charles, preserver of England's peace and begetter of her splendid new prosperity—might live.

The King recovered—his marvellous constitution saved him both from his illness and the doctor's remedies—and he knew that at last the tide had begun to turn against his enemies. In the last months of 1680 the old Catholic peer Lord Stafford was tried for treason and condemned. Charles could do nothing to aid him without flouting the laws of the land, except commute his sentence to beheading. Shaftesbury, Russell, Sidney and the rest of the pack howled for the full sentence—hanging, disembowelling, and quartering—but this the King would not permit. The old man died for his faith with exemplary fortitude, but his death, Catholic though he was, returned like a boomerang upon his false accusers. The people knew him to be blameless, except for his religion, and that the evidence given at his trial was one long tissue of lies by Shaftesbury's paid informers. Slowly their sanity was returning, and their sense of indignation aroused against the Terrorists. Gradually, at last, they began to turn towards the King in the realization that through all these years of panic and persecution he alone had kept a level head, standing firm and unbowed in the darkest hours for toleration, justice, fair-dealing.

Thus in March, '81, when he dissolved his last Parliament at Oxford, there was no angry outburst by the nation as a whole; for the moment the majority were content to stand apart, watching the duel between Shaftesbury and the King.

The following months Charles took the offensive. Far too long he had suffered abuse and defamation in those scurrilous pamphlets which were the newspapers of the day. Now he replied by issuing a newspaper of his own, *The Observator,* in which he unmasked the designs of the conspirators and explained his policy to the people. It was a stroke of genius; eagerly the publication was seized upon and read by all. In a few months the Tory leaders had followed suit, and Shaftesbury's envenomed propaganda was being countered by a thousand angry pamphlets from the pens of writers for the Crown.

Charles now felt himself strong enough to deal with the informers. One after another these idols of the London mob were seized and brought before him, rigorously examined, their lies unmasked, and dealt with according to their deserts. Then one July morning he left Windsor in the greatest secrecy before dawn, arrived in London by nine o'clock, arrested Shaftesbury in his bed, and seized his papers. By evening Charles was back at Windsor, with no disturbance but the snarling of the mob.

The papers proved beyond all doubt that Shaftesbury was implicated in a plot to overthrow both King and Government. In November he was brought to trial, but the devilish machinery by which he had subverted justice saved him. The rabble stormed the Old Bailey, howled down the judges, and stoned the witnesses for the Crown; while a jury packed by the Whig Sheriffs secured the acquittal of their leader. Yet Charles had the last word, for he published the demagogue's papers, and after that, except for the scum of the streets and his fellow conspirators, Shaftesbury lost all credit. In the following year he sought refuge in Holland—a dying, embittered, and broken man.

It was largely through Shaftesbury's creation of the Liberal Party, who inherited his hatred of Charles, that so much unjustified vilification has adhered to the wise, tolerant King. But the evidence against the bitter Earl remains for all to read in the trials of those thousands of poor people who suffered at the hands of his packed juries and through the false accusations of his iniquitous informers. Dryden, who knew him, has preserved the true portrait of this arch-traitor for posterity:

> 'A name to all succeeding ages cursed,
> For close designs and crooked councils fit
> Sagacious, bold and turbulent of wit . . .
> In friendship false, implacable in hate,
> Resolved to Ruin, or to Rule the State.'

Charles now prepared to attack that last stronghold of sedition—the City. He was determined that at all costs justice in the law courts should be restored, and proceeded against the City Charter with a writ of 'Quo Warranto'. During the Whig tyranny the citizens had been forced by a hostile crowd to poll for Shaftesbury's nominees at the election of the Sheriffs. Now, with the assistance of a loyal Lord Mayor, Charles drove away the mob and made possible a free election. Two loyalists were returned by a sweeping majority and the Whigs thrown out, so at last juries could again be chosen irrespective of the politics, and justice was restored to London Town.

The Whigs died hard, but now, without a Parliament to hamper him and with his loyal press bringing his motives more clearly before the people, England was at last coming to understand the King and value him at his true worth. James was brought home, Catholics and Dissenters given a more reasonable liberty, and all the while England grew richer with the constant arrival of her merchant fleets.

It was not till '83 that Charles became supreme, and that through a well-planned attempt upon his life. He had been to Newmarket, as was his custom in the spring, for he loved his horses, the racing, and the country air, but he was forced to return to London earlier than he had planned, owing to a serious stable fire. A few days later he was made acquainted with the details of a plot against his life. Forty fanatics, mostly old Cromwellian troopers, had planned to hold up his coach at the 'Rye House', near Ware, on the date originally fixed for his return. But for their premature departure owing to the fire, both James and he would have been assassinated.

The conspiracy, however, was far more widespread than this. Upon the news of his death, Monmouth, Russell, Essex, Sidney and the rest of the Whig Lords were to seize Whitehall and form a Regency. It was Shaftesbury's last attack, engineered by him from Holland. The ringleaders were seized, a true bill being found against twenty-one persons. Essex cut his throat in the Tower, Russell and Sidney went to the scaffold. Yet such was Charles' generosity of nature that in both instances he commuted their sentence to beheading, observing of the former 'that he would not deny him that courtesy which he had endeavoured to withhold from the innocent Stafford', and sent him a message before he died 'that his confiscated estates should be restored to his wife and children'.

Once again Charles published the evidence, that all might be acquainted with the details of the plot, and then the true feelings of the people were made manifest. The rebellious Whigs were scattered and the voice of the nation rose in a pæan of thanksgiving for the preservation of the King. All who had ever come into contact with him knew his tolerant spirit, his unfailing kindness and generosity; 'a man who liked to be easy and see those about him so'. He had brought England out of anarchy and chaos to law and order, and never at any time in her history had Britain been so prosperous before. Money was pouring into the country from every land and clime. Ships could not be built quick enough to cope with the increasing commerce. A new and better London had risen from the ashes of the old. Fine manor houses were rising up in every village of the kingdom. There was ample employment and money for all. From the richest to the poorest a higher standard of living had become the order of the day, and to that smiling England it seemed that the golden age had come at last.

To one tall, dark ageing *roué* the credit for all this happiness was due. 'Better one King than five hundred,' he had declared when he dismissed that last Parliament as 'A House of Talkers'. And how can we ignore the verdict of that happy, prosperous England, for which he had striven so hard throughout all his reign, and that had become an actual fact during the last years of 'despotism'?

In the loving hearts of his people, their devotion and enthusiasm, Charles—reigning without a Parliament—stands justified.

EIGHT

The Apotheosis

DURING the last years Charles was a poor man. It was the old business of no Parliament—no money; but he cut down his household, lived mostly in the country for economy's sake, and managed quite happily on the French subsidies.

The feeling of loyalty in these years was so great that no less than sixty-five boroughs voluntarily surrendered their Charters to the King that they might be amended in such a manner that they could never again be used by another Shaftesbury to subvert justice in the interests of a political party.

One trouble remained. His beloved, empty-headed son, who had so foolishly allowed himself to be made a puppet by the conspirators. For the time, Monmouth was sent abroad in disgrace, but, before he died, Charles had made arrangements to recall and pardon him.

James gained reflected glory from the King's popularity. His courage and fine work as Lord High Admiral were recalled, and the throne assured to him upon his brother's death. Yet that Charles was uneasy as to what troubles James' bigoted Catholicism might lead him into is shown by the confidence which he made to Sir Richard Bulstrode. 'I am weary,' he said, 'of travelling, and am resolved to go abroad no more. But when I am dead and gone, I know not what my brother will do: I am much afraid that when he comes to wear the crown he will be obliged to travel again. And yet I will take care to leave my kingdoms to him in peace, wishing he may long keep them so. But this hath all my fears, little of my hopes, and less of my reason.' Time was to show how right that master-mind was in its shrewd judgment.

He expressed the same view in a more jovial manner when, after the Rye House Plot, James became nervous for his safety. 'Fear not, James; they will never kill me to make thee King.'

From time to time he received deputations and petitions asking him to call a Parliament, but he would never venture upon those troubled waters again, and to one collection of Berkshire Brewers who approached him on the matter his reply was typical of his tactful methods. 'Gentlemen,' he said amiably, 'brewing is your concern and governing mine, and I wonder that my neighbours should meddle with my business, but we will argue the matter over a cup of your good ale when next we meet at Windsor'—and thus another batch of malcontents were turned from enemies to friends.

He still remained hale and hearty as the years advanced, walking ten miles of a morning over Newmarket Heath or spending long days in the more restful pastime of fishing Dachet Reach, which was a very favourite spot with him. Journeys of inspection to the Fleet were frequent, and always a great pleasure to him. Pepys, the one-time poor relation of Sir Edward Montagu, was now amassing his fine library, and was his sovereign's old and trusted friend. Charles had himself assumed the post of Lord High Admiral and the honest Samuel was his right-hand man.

The King also exercised his small but well-trained Army which he had increased as much as his straitened circumstances would allow. To the already established Coldstream, Blues, Royal Scots, and Buffs he had added a regiment of Grenadiers, two troops of Life Guards, the Royal Dragoons, the Queen's Regiment and the Scots' Greys—and he particularly concerned himself that their arms should be of the very latest pattern. Bayonets were invented which did away with the necessity for pikemen to protect the musketeers, clumsy old powder horns abolished, and cartridges introduced. In Chelsea, at the suggestion of Sir Stephen Fox, then Paymaster of the Forces, he established the hospital for old soldiers, and at Greenwich he personally conducted those experiments which led to hand grenades and the filling of hitherto solid cannon balls with gunpowder which converted them into the forerunner of the modern shell. His interest in science never flagged, and many experiments were always in progress in his own laboratory.

On Sundays he attended church and, although he was by no means a religious man, listened to the sermons of his divines with interest. To one impertinent who took advantage of his well-known good nature to upbraid him from the pulpit for the irregularities of his private life he sent a message. 'Tell him,' he said gently, 'that I am not angry to be told my faults, but would have it done in a gentlemanly like manner.' He often afterwards commented upon the sermons, saying of one preacher that 'He had played the fool upon the doctrine of purgatory' and of another, 'He gave us quite an unnecessary sermon on the doctrine of original sin,' and he made Thomas Ken Bishop of Bath and Wells for the gentle, saintly way in which he remonstrated with him for his sins. In fact, at no time in the history of England have the high offices of the Church been filled with so many saintly and scholarly divines, worthy in every way of their position, as in his reign. The personal selection of all these men was one of the King's most closely guarded privileges.

William Penn, a religious of a different persuasion, came to see Charles at Whitehall on one occasion. This stalwart Quaker disapproved of kings and Charles II in particular, therefore he remained covered in his presence. Charles, never at a loss, removed his own befeathered headgear with that graceful sweep of which he was such a master. Penn, looking ill at ease, enquired, 'Why dost thou remove thy hat, Charles Stuart?' 'Because, Penn, it is the custom here for only one person to remain covered at the time,' smiled the King, and, having administered this gentlest of rebukes, he took the Quaker by the arm and led him in, spread out the charts and gave his able brain to the task of assisting Penn in the foundation of the great State of Pennsylvania.

The Court was no longer youthful and a quieter merriment prevailed. Buckingham had retired long since to his estates, disgusted by the ill success of his intrigues against a kindly master. There he gave himself to hunting and hobnobbing with the villagers. Once when the innkeeper told him that he was in a plaguy hurry for his morning draught we find recorded a flash of his old spontaneous wit:

> '"Some Ale! Some Ale," the impetuous Villiers cried,
> To which the surly Landlord thus replied,
> "Plague on your Grace, you treat me as your dog,
> I'll serve your Lordship when I've served my Hog."'

But the glory was departed. In his last years that restless brain turned to religion, and he published *A Short Discourse upon the Reasonableness of Man's having a Religion and Worship of God*. Finally he became morbidly anxious as to the state of his soul and, having caught a chill out hunting, died in 1688 at the village inn, surrounded by the local clergy but regretted by none.

For years the gay and dissolute Rochester had drunk enough each day to intoxicate six ordinary men, and, although it had never appeared to affect him at the time, it ruined his constitution and in the end, and at the age of thirty he retired from court an old and dying man. He made his bitter swan song in 1680.

> 'Tir'd with the noisome Follies of the Age,
> And weary of my part, I quit the Stage,
> For who in life's dull Farce a part would bear,
> Where Rogues, Whores, Bawds, all the head Actors are?'

In his decline he trained the great Mrs. Barry for the stage, having unquenchable faith in her genius. At her first appearance she was voted the worst actress in the kingdom, but his faith was justified, for in the end she became the greatest tragedienne of her time. Rochester's life among his family does something to redeem his otherwise shameful existence. He also turned to religion in the end and made a most edifying exit in the same summer as his retirement.

Sedley had become more serious and sat in Charles' last Parliament. He was to survive the King by sixteen years, and to his intense annoyance James took his daughter, Catherine, for his mistress. 'I hate ingratitude,' declared the reformed rake on hearing this, 'and therefore, as the King has made *my* daughter a Countess—I will endeavour to make *his* daughter a Queen.' And he did—by assisting in the bringing over of William and Mary.

It was Catherine Sedley, Countess of Dorchester, who, as an old, old lady in the time of George I, came upon the even more aged Portsmouth and the then elderly Lady Orkney—who had been William III's mistress—at a party, and electrified the company by exclaiming, 'Well! Well! Well! Who would have thought to find three old whores like us in the same house?'

The son of Sedley's old friend D'Avernant, the theatrical magnate, was with him in his last hours, and said that he died like a true philosopher, 'without fear or superstition'.

'Gentle George' Etheridge lingered on at Court and after the King's death secured an appointment as British Ambassador to Ratisbon. He had gained some little diplomatic experience as secretary to our Ambassador at the Porte in '68, which had brought forth the couplet:

> 'Ovid to Pontus sent for too much wit,
> Etheridge to Turkey for the want of it.'

He set out for Ratisbon with the light-hearted irresponsibility which characterized all his actions, and at the

Hague got so drunk that he passed the whole night unconscious in the streets—the only recorded instance of a representative accredited by the Court of St. James behaving in so unambassadorial a manner. At Ratisbon the gay George found the heavy Germans incredibly dull, so he spent most of his time in the more congenial atmosphere of the French Embassy. He carried on a considerable correspondence with Dryden and the other wits, maintaining an unflagging interest in the theatre. To his old companions he wrote a little sadly, recalling the joys of other days, as on one occasion, 'Remind my Lord Dorset how he and I carried two draggle-tail nymphs one bitter frosty night over the Thames to Lambeth.' But that Etheridge was something more than a rake and drunkard is seen from his charming verse:

'Upon the downs when shall I breathe at ease,
Have nothing else to do but what I please.
In a fresh cooling shade upon the bank
Of Arden's spring, have time to read and think,
And stretch, and sleep, when all my cares shall be
For Health, and pleasure my philosophy?
When shall I rest from business, noise and strife,
Lay down the soldier's and the courtier's life
And in a little melancholy seat
Begin at last to live and to forget
The nonsense and the farce of what the fools call great?'

In '89 he left Ratisbon to spend his declining years in the Paris that he loved. In '91 he died, a poet of no mean ability but unregenerate to the last.

Dorset, or Buckhurst, as he was in the days when Pretty, Witty Nelly came to town, had become more sober with advancing years and took upon his shoulders those burdens of the State which became his rank. He remained a true friend to Charles until the latter's death, and then was prominent in the bringing over of William of Orange. Later he held the great office of Lord Chamberlain, and died full of years and honours at Bath in 1706, perhaps the most magnificent patron of the Arts that England has ever known.

And now we come to the death of the man who stood head and shoulders above them all, who—if he was the chief figure at their gay suppers and encouraged their licence for his recreation—was also in the quiet hours the greatest diplomat and statesman of his time.

When the King rose on the morning of February 2nd, 1685, he was far from well. He had not been in his usual health for some days, and now his attendants were alarmed at his condition. He was pale, vague in his movements, and seemed to understand ill what those about him said. Half an hour later, while being shaved, he had a fit. He was immediately blooded, and all those drastic, exhausting measures which the medicine of the age considered requisite were applied. All through that morning, afternoon, and evening, clysters, poultices, and purgatives were forced upon the unresisting King. At two o'clock the following morning he fell into an uneasy sleep. At dawn they woke him to see how he was getting on. He was sane and conscious and throughout Tuesday submitted with unfailing patience to the doctors' renewed attacks. By nightfall he was well enough to send a last message to the greatest of his servants, the old and trusty Ormonde.

In the meantime the news of the King's seizure had been spread abroad. Consternation and dismay gripped the hearts of his subjects. A terrible hush fell upon the City, and a vast multitude assembled outside the palace gates. Kneeling in the streets, or standing mute and unashamed with tears coursing down their cheeks, the people watched and prayed. Charles stood for peace, for justice and fair-dealing; what would happen if he were to be taken from them? In these last years they had come to know him as their one defence against the tyranny of faction and the greed of self-seeking demagogues. It was a personal fear and sorrow as though some big, kindly, understanding brother had been stricken down.

On Wednesday morning Charles was very weak, but better, then in the evening he relapsed, breaking into a cold, clammy sweat. The fourteen doctors in attendance, pressed by the Council as to the King's malady, called it 'intermittent fever', but in the light of modern knowledge we know that it was an attack brought on by chronic

Bright's disease. By midday Thursday a terrible change had occurred—Charles had gone black in the face, was in great pain, and writhing in convulsions. They now realized that there could be no hope of his recovery.

The waiting clergy knelt beside his bed, begging him to receive the last rites of the Protestant Communion. He thanked them and spoke of his sorrow for his sins, yet turned away, even from his dear friend 'little Ken', but Louise de Queroalle knew his need although she could not be beside him. She spoke urgently to Barillion, the French Ambassador, and begged him to speak to York. The Duke agreed and in a whisper asked the King 'Was it his wish to be received into the Roman Communion?' 'Yes—with all my heart,' was the dying man's reply. James cleared the Royal bedchamber and smuggled in a Catholic priest. By the strangest of coincidences it was that same Father Huddlestone who more than thirty years before had led the fugitive Charles through the stormy night to the shelter and safety of Mosley.

To Huddlestone Charles said that he wished to be absolved of the sins of his past life, for which he was truly sorry, that he pardoned his enemies, and begging pardon of those whom he had offended. He then made full and sincere confession and afterwards received the Sacrament, thus acknowledging at the last that doctrine of salvation which of all Christian faiths is still the most widely accepted throughout the world.

From ten o'clock that night, when he received extreme unction, until the following morning, he remained conscious and spoke clearly. To York, who was weeping unrestrainedly, he spoke of his love for him as a brother, and begged him to overlook all his actions against him that might have seemed unkind, for he had been forced to them. To him, also, he recommended the care of his wife and children.

At midnight that poor, barren lady the Queen, to whom, despite his many infidelities, he had through all the years been so steadfast a protector, came to say farewell. She was distraught with grief and so overcome at the thought of losing him that she had to be carried fainting from the room. Later she sent to ask pardon for her weakness. 'Alas, poor woman,' replied the dying King, '*she* asks my pardon? *I* beg hers with all my heart: take her back that answer.'

With the Bishops and Great Officers of State kneeling about him, he raised himself up in his bed, asked God's blessing upon his people, and prayed that they would pardon him if in anything he had not been a good King.

Once he asked the time and, on being told, remarked, 'My business will soon be done.' Then he spoke to York once more, begging him to have a care for Louise and the children—and 'Let not poor Nelly starve.'

Although in great pain, he continued to submit to the ministrations of his doctors with a marvellous fortitude, and once, with a flash of the old humour, observed, 'Gentlemen, I beg you to pardon me for being such an unconscionable time in dying.'

At the coming of dawn he asked the time again, and bid them 'Open the curtains that I may once more see the light of day.' For a little he lay still while the brightness of the February morning flooded the tall chamber. By ten o'clock he had lapsed into unconsciousness and the great spirit was free at last.

All England mourned him, whatever might be their Creed. Rough sailors upon the high seas, the grooms and jockeys of the racing stables, merchants, scientists, men of letters. The actors at the theatre, the watermen upon the Thames, those saintly Divines whom he had so carefully selected, no less than the wits to whom he had been a boon companion, and the little Army which he had reared, later to earn such laurels under Marlborough. To one and all he had proved himself a master worth the serving, and the loyallest of friends.

Nothing can better show his unfailing courage and gently kind nature than the repetition of a few of his own sayings which have come down to us.

'Had I but ten thousand good and loyal soldiers and subjects, I would soon drive all these rogues forth out of my Kingdom.' . . . 'I am weary of hanging—let it rest.' . . . 'I will take care to leave my Kingdoms to him in peace, wishing he may long keep them so.' . . . 'They think that

I am anxious for a divorce, but I will not see an innocent woman abused.' . . . 'I will never use arbitrary Government myself, and am resolved not to suffer it in others.' . . . 'Let not poor Nelly starve.'

He was a very human man, a good-natured *roué*—who seeks to deny it?—but, owing to his constant habit of jesting, his intellect has been underrated. He was undoubtedly the cleverest and perhaps the greatest man who ever sat upon the English throne.

For two hundred years his character has been belittled as a definite policy against the weak and inept Pretenders who succeeded in the Stuart line. The legend that he was nothing but an idle, dissipated Monarch dies hard. Yet in the constant sifting of the sieve of time the dross of libel falls away, leaving the gold of truth revealed. The day will come when Charles will take his rightful place in history as the wise, sweet-natured King who led his people out of darkness, anarchy and persecution into the Great Prosperity of the Georgian Century.

BIBLIOGRAPHICAL NOTE

THIS short volume does not pretend to be anything but a sketch of 'Old Rowley himself', with, I trust, sufficient of those interests and personalities which filled the background of his life to give some idea of the pressures which were brought to bear upon him, his motives, failures and achievements.

It would be idle to list all the volumes which I have read, since others more learned—writing on the same period—have read and listed all of them, and many more.

The following, therefore, should only be taken as a guide by those who come fresh to the subject, and in whom the present book has been fortunate enough to raise a desire for further knowledge of Charles II and his times.

Before any other, I would suggest that remarkable achievement *King Charles II* by Arthur Bryant. With monumental erudition Mr. Bryant has given us a long and detailed history of the reign, and his bibliography will supply the most voracious reader with material for many years to come. Do not imagine, however, that his work is a dull tale of dates and charters. His prose is beautiful

—there is not a single dull page in the book—and for our delight he makes the long-dead King, with his courtiers and courtesans, live once again.

Among the most outstanding of the original sources are: Clarendon's *History of the Great Rebellion* and Burnet's *History of My Own Times*—long, heavy sometimes, but authoritative.

The later historians, Gardiner, Hume and Ranke, in their respective *Histories of England*, discourse at length in the scholastic manner, and Strickland's *Lives of the Queens of England* gives the story from a slightly different angle.

Then we have the diarists—often inaccurate regarding affairs of state, but unparalleled for pictures of life as it was lived in those days—the delightful and so human Pepys, the sober and somewhat pompous Evelyn, together with the *Letters* of Madame de Sévigné, which make excellent reading.

The *Memoirs* of the Comte de Gramont stand unrivalled for their portrayal of the amorous scandals of the Court, and those of Lady Fanshawe make an interesting study.

On the more serious side, Keith Feiling's two books, *A History of the Tory Party* and *British Foreign Policy, 1660-1672*, with Sir George Sitwell's *The First Whig*, give an excellent exposition of the political and foreign situations which arose during the reign.

BIBLIOGRAPHICAL NOTE

Allan Fea's *After Worcester Fight* and *The Flight of the King* are now accepted as giving the best account of Charles' epic escape, while hunted across England by his enemies, and in Eva Scott's *Travels of the King* will be found the full story of his exile.

Saintsbury's *Dryden* and the Nonsuch *Wycherley* give, in addition to the works of these leading dramatists, great variety of information upon the theatre and its denizens in those hectic days which succeeded the Restoration; and the Nonsuch *Rochester* not only gives all the verse but an admirable life of that versatile scamp.

E. Barrington Chancellor's *Lives of the Rakes*, Vols. I and II, give slight but informative sketches of the principal courtiers and mistresses, and Mr. P. Cunningham's *Story of Nell Gwynn and Sayings of Charles II* will tell the reader quite a lot about the so-called 'Merry Monarch's' domestic muddles.

'And so to bed.'

D. W.

INDEX

INDEX

G

H

INDEX

INDEX

Q

R

INDEX

INDEX